About the author

Photo: © Jon Dennis

Noor Hibbert is a qualified life and business coach, serial-entrepreneur, motivational speaker, author, mother and spiritual badass.

Noor has a degree in Psychology and Postgraduate Certifications in Business & Executive Coaching and Coaching Psychology.

She is a trained Strategic Intervention coach and Rapid Transformational Therapist.

She is the proud founder of This Is Your Dream – where she helps people transform their mindset, master manifestation and live their best life through her monthly memberships.

She also supports people in building their business in her coaching programs and is the host of the 'Think It, Get It' podcast.

She has built a seven figure business whilst raising three small children and she strongly believes that embarking on a spiritual journey has accelerated her success.

You Only Live Once

I

Shit-Faced + Shoeless

As I looked at each digit on the screen in front of me and blinked as though it could be a mistake, it dawned on me – I had completely and utterly changed my life.

I was looking at the money that little old me had made over the last four years, and it had surpassed a million fine English pounds. One freaking million. But this money was more than just seven digits on a screen; it was a representation of how I'd gone from a mere desire to change my life to this very moment writing this book for you.

My name is Noor and ten years ago, at the age of 24, I can assure you that I was not living the life I had imagined I would have been by my mid-twenties. I was more 'hot mess' rather than life success.

At 24, I thought I'd have been in some fancy job in London (that I'd got as a result of outstanding university results), living in Chelsea, one hundred per cent madly in love with a man who just adored every single part of me, and possibly with a litter of children.

Instead, I was completely shit-faced, walking barefoot down the bar-lined strip in Ibiza, surrounded by young people excitedly drinking from neon pink fishbowls as they planned their night of debauchery on the White Isle. I was with my friend Alan, and because I was so drunk and kept falling arse over tit with the heels I was wearing, Alan did what any good gay friend would do, he took my beautiful three-inch high-heel shoes and threw them into some random field. Curiously, there was a field nestled in the back streets of San Antonio, or perhaps it was someone's garden. Who knows? As I said, I was shit-faced and shoeless.

My level of intoxication was the result of a semi-celebration of being single and finally being out of an 18-month-long relationship with Mr Wrong 6.0, and partly in mourning for the fact I was still freaking clueless about how I was going to meet Prince Charming. So I did what any self-respecting 24-year-old who lived in Ibiza did – I went out and drank my body weight in Jägerbombs. I think it's probably a good thing to give you some context of how I ended up there on the said strip in Ibiza with Alan – my angry, shoe-throwing, Scottish gay friend.

I grew up in a tiny three-bed house on a council estate in South West London. My parents met very young, and as my Iranian mother had never been taught about the perils of unprotected sex (sex was not talked about in the Middle East!), she fell pregnant with me at 18 years old. This was BAD news. My parents were both Middle Eastern so having a child out of wedlock was worse than… in fact there was actually nothing in the world that it was worse than!

So after my dad tried to convince her to have an abortion, which she refused, they went for the next best option – get married and live unhappily ever after till death did them part. My parents were young, and they both did what they felt was *right*, dictated by social and cultural norms, but they already decided the fate of me as an innocent foetus and I was destined to live in a household built on a loveless marriage for the following decade. I can tell you that this is a recipe for disaster when it comes to bringing up a healthy, functioning human being.

And then, as if they never learned the first time, my sister was born ten months later. Yes, ten months. The reason being that my poor mother had been diagnosed with cancer while pregnant with me. Following treatment after my birth, she unintentionally fell pregnant once again, but due to the treatment she was undergoing, my sister arrived at the 26-week mark of her pregnancy at just 2lb 1oz. For a child to survive such an early birth is honestly a miracle, and my poor parents couldn't bring her home for six months as she innocently lay in an incubator, fighting for her life.

My mum worked every hour she could to make sure we would survive, spending time between me and my sister in the hospital as babies. Because, as if life wasn't hard enough for her, at 12 months old, I decided to completely stop eating and was also put in hospital. My parents now had two children in hospital and were both very young and trying to make ends meet. The reason I'm telling you this is because, later on, we are going to talk about the impact of our upbringing and I think it's only fair you get to see that I wasn't born into some magical, completely functioning family and got to where I am today because of that. I want to show you that in fact from the moment I was born, things were not easy in my little life.

Fast-forward and off I went to a regular state school in white suburban London. At the age of four, a girl told me I was ugly and questioned why I had such bushy brows. It became very apparent to me from that moment that I was different from all the white English people in my school and, no matter how much I tried, I was never going to blend in with a name like Noor. This feeling of being an outsider plagued me for many years after that incident to the point that I begged my mum if I could change my name via deed poll.

By the time I was nine I had such a thick South West London accent, and had lost my ability to use the letter 'h' at the beginning of any sentence, that my dad decided we needed to go to private schools. At this point, my dad was a practising lawyer and my mother worked as a manager for a care home.

Although this decision financially pushed my parents to the limit, education is a strong value in Middle Eastern families and so, while we didn't have a luxurious life by any stretch of the imagination, they both decided to send us to a private school. This would, of course, be the golden ticket for us to go off and get the successful career that my parents had envisioned for us.

I joined at age ten, and stayed in private education till I finished my A-levels. However, it became evident quickly as I embarked on a private school education that at every step of the way we were flung into competition with one another, and at every corner there was an opportunity to feel 'less than' everybody else.

Even after years of attending an all-girls private school, despite my unshakable desire to be cool and fit in, I never quite made the cut.

I wasn't sporty so didn't get onto any of the sports teams.

I wasn't academic so never won any of the accolades that came alongside that.

I couldn't play an instrument particularly well nor, despite my sheer determination, would I ever get the main parts in the school plays; I was painfully average at everything and found the whole process of trying to come top at anything very hard.

I wish I could erase the memory of the dreaded day me and my classmates had to take our cycling proficiency test; a test to determine if you were able to cycle on a road, without a road in sight. I rocked up on my new purple BMX bike, proud as punch, ready to show them that I could indeed indicate left and right with my hand gestures while keeping my balance on this sexy little vehicle on the fake roads drawn out in chalk across the school playground.

At the end of the day, I was one of only two people that had completely failed. Looking back on it, I have to ask myself 'How the f*** is it even possible to fail at cycling in a playground?' They didn't even let me have another go to pass the test. After that day I had been relegated from the non-cool club to Sub-Zero Loserville in my head. *It's fine*, I told myself. I would learn to drive before any of them and then stick a middle finger up when I saw them cycling up Wimbledon Hill.

At the age of 12, my parents finally divorced. Unlike most children who mourn the breakup of their parents, I was happy. We had lived in a toxic environment for over a decade and finally we could just be with my mum who let us do what we wanted. My dad was incredibly strict and his rules were suffocating to a free spirit like me. I missed out on sleepovers, parties, and that one amazing school ski trip to the USA that everyone bar me went on. Oh the humiliation! I used to hope that everyone had the worst time and never wanted to talk about it when they came home, but, for weeks after, everyone had all these insider jokes and memories because, of course, a ski trip to the USA at 11 years old was fucking fabulous and I missed out.

My school life got worse before it got better. In year 7, I got so badly bullied that at some points I truly wished that I was dead. The humiliating memory of walking up during lunch time to sit at a table to be told by Emma (the bully) that I couldn't sit there because I would give everyone germs, has been forever etched on my Soul. My mere existence irritated Emma so much that she made it her mission to make me feel like I didn't belong. I never wanted to do anything to try and upset her and to this day I'll never know what it was about me that made her feel the need to bully me. The hardest part was when I told my mum I wanted to move school, and she said no. I don't think she ever realized the gravitas of the situation. It's very hard as parents to remember how everything feels as a child. I felt helpless – which unfortunately is one of the prerequisites for depression.

A few years passed and, thank goodness, I started to blossom from this awkward child into a girl. I found tweezers (goodbye monobrow) and was one of the first of my friends to grow boobs. Suddenly I was attractive to boys and I got my first boyfriend at 14. Suddenly I had something to offer the girls (including the bully): a group of boys to hang around with (and now no reason to get bullied). I had waited years for this moment, because I'd heard the stories of all the cool girls having their first snogs at school. That word makes me shudder now, but getting a snog is literally the pinnacle of school life when you're at an all-girl school at the age of 13.

But as quickly as that romance started, I suffered my first excruciating heartbreak. At the age of 15 I was dumped by the first love of my life, after four months of courting, via text message no less. And the worst part was that after the text he sent to dump me, he accidentally sent a text to me that was meant for the girl he dumped me for – a girl who people said looked similar to me, but had longer hair, a better body and was prettier.

I started to struggle with my mental health again after this, but found a glimmer of hope when I ended up dating a boy five years older than me. I felt like I'd arrived into womanhood with a bang, even though I had completely lied about his age to my mum and stepdad. I felt mature dating this older guy, my school kudos had now escalated as he would pick me up from school in his little white

Citroën AX and I would wave my school friends goodbye as though I'd won the boyfriend lottery. *I was so goddamn cool.* The way I felt, you would have thought he was driving an Aston Martin and treating me to Michelin star meals instead of 16 nuggets at Wandsworth McDonald's drive-through – but I didn't care as long as he loved me.

At the start it was magical. We would take drives down to Brighton and sleep overlooking the sea on the tiny back seat of his car, listening to Heart radio's late-night love songs. I loved being in love, but things started to take a nasty turn about six months in. He started to become controlling, jealous and would cause me pain for no reason. I was only 16 and, because I was in love, I didn't understand that he was emotionally and mentally abusing me. I was talking to one of his friends in the local Wetherspoon's pub, and he thought I was flirting, so he came over and threw a pint of beer all over me and told me that now nobody would fancy me.

If I tried to see friends he would make me feel guilty and he would purposely ignore me for days to torture me in his absence, leaving me wondering what he was doing. The emotional abuse got worse and worse and it all came to a head one winter's day, when I told him I wanted to go to a party with my school friends. He tried to commit suicide and told me it was my fault and that if I ever left him he would do it again.

I had been going through a lot of stuff that I've chosen to not share publicly, but life was too much for me at this point. I went to the doctor's and she prescribed me Prozac just days before my 17th birthday. There was no one to talk to, no one who understood and I felt ashamed that I'd got so low and I needed medication. On my 17th birthday he promised my mum that he had organized something for me and for her not to plan a party. I waited hours after school. He never turned up. He would make an excuse and each time I'd fall for it, each time wondering why I was so unlovable and forgettable that he couldn't even be bothered to remember my birthday.

One night, his temper got worse and he physically hurt me. That was the day we broke up, and a few months after that I stopped taking the anti-depressants. And a few months after that I met James. James was kind, funny, loving – the perfect boyfriend and for the first time in a long time I felt *really* happy. I was completely in love.

As the year passed, school started to feel easier even though academically I found it a challenge. I managed to get into my top university choice; thank goodness for my photographic memory otherwise I'm not sure I would have got into any university!

The crazy thing is I never wanted to go to university to study something like Psychology. In fact, studying anything remotely science-y was about as appealing as swallowing a bit of sick that accidentally ends up in your throat. Ever since I was a little girl I wanted to be a performer of some sort or a writer. I was a creative person, so it was shocking to even me that I would go to get a degree that would make me a Bachelor of Science.

Years earlier, my dreams of being on Broadway were quashed after a 'realistic' conversation with a career advisor. After that conversation, I decided that I quite fancied being a criminal psychologist. I got lost in a daydream that somehow my life would be like an episode of *CSI*, and that perhaps I'd end up in some fancy documentary on Sky and then get promoted and shipped over to the USA to work for the FBI. Yes, that's exactly what would happen. I was going to work for the FBI.

That was the train of thought in my 17-year-old head that landed me at Cardiff University to study Psychology. The prospect of being some sort of secret agent wearing a Chanel suit and high heels, being applauded by people for how fantastic I was that I'd managed to see through The Psychopath's lies was enough to push me through my A-levels.

James and I started Cardiff University together, with big dreams of a long future together. However, within the first term I was delivered the devastating news that Criminal Psychology had been dropped as an option and all my dreams of working for the FBI were cruelly swept from underneath me in an instant. It was probably a good thing with hindsight, because I didn't really have much time for studying at university. There were much more important things to do, such as attend every single fun event at the student union on a weekly basis.

University exists in some sort of parallel universe where, instead of just going out on the weekends (like in my previous 'normal' life), it was perfectly acceptable (and even applauded) to wake up with a hangover on any night of the week. If I wasn't going to work for the FBI or be on Broadway, I might as well go out and get ridiculously drunk. This was my antidote to dealing with the anxiety I'd started to develop since I was 17 and the cracks that were starting to show in my relationship with James.

By the end of the second term, it became evident to me that I had chosen the completely wrong degree. They should have never let me in. I was nowhere near smart enough to ever pass. Trying to construct scientific research papers doing advanced degree-level Maths and Statistics made me want to vomit. Did they not know I'd only got a B at Maths GCSE because I got extra help after being put in some random special group for people that were so bad at maths we weren't even allowed to take maths with the rest of the class!? And here I was sitting doing a level of Maths at university designed for geniuses. I would cry every time I looked at the papers because I genuinely felt so thick and lost.

I remember the day that I got on the phone to my mum and begged to leave university – in the same way that I had begged to leave school. Not only was I struggling with studies, my darling boyfriend decided to end it with me after two years because he wanted to be single at uni. I'm pretty sure if someone had smashed me in the ribs with a sledgehammer it would have been less painful than hearing that news.

I wanted to run away, but my mum convinced me that I should stay and stick it out, and that she would get me a tutor to help with the maths, and that I would soon move on and heal from the horrendous breakup. To be honest, the one thing that kept me there at university was my best friend Lucy, who I'd met on day one of my life in halls of residence. After all those years at school so desperately wishing for the connection that the other girls had, I finally knew what it meant to have a female friend who truly was your best friend. We were neighbours, and from the minute she said. 'Let's go across the road and get a beer in the pub', I knew that we would be soul sisters forever.

I could be completely me around her and she loved and supported me through so many of my dark times. She was also studying Psychology, and we lived together for the next three years. Considering performing was now off the cards and I wasn't going to end up on *CSI*, I needed a Plan B. But since I didn't have a Plan B, I decided for now escaping real life and spending the summer working as a Club 18–30 holiday rep was a phenomenal idea.

I had intently watched the series *Club Reps* when I was 13 years old and just intuitively knew that I wanted to go and be one. In February of 2006, I went to my first interview in sunny Bradford, nervous in anticipation of what was going to happen next. Would this city unveil the next chapter of my life working on sunny shores, allowing me to escape the heartbreak of my failed relationships, a Psychology degree I would never pass and the grey skies of Wales?

I was 19 years old when I received the letter that I had got the job. I was over the moon. I had never felt so excited about anything. I needed to escape because the heartbreak was bad enough, but when you go to uni with your boyfriend and make a group of friends as a couple, it means that you see your ex out everywhere. The worst part was after he broke up with me, he would constantly end up getting drunk, telling me he loved me and wanting me back, to just cruelly change his mind the following morning. I needed to escape the never-ending pain, and a debauched summer away was exactly what the doctor ordered.

In June 2006 I landed on the sunny shores of Malia, Greece, to spend my first summer working as a holiday rep. I can categorically tell you that the TV series did not show the gruelling hours, the lack of sleep or the amount of selling that you would do to unsuspecting holiday makers at three o'clock in the morning. Nor did it show you that you would end up putting on a stone in weight as a result of red vodka and kebabs, which would intensify my already dwindling relationship with my body. But I also made incredible memories and grew more resilient as a person.

However, I came back after that summer and vowed I'd never go again. I was so exhausted. Sometimes I was that sleep deprived, I would try to take a nap while I was walking between seeing holiday makers. Fast-forward a year later, just like the surreal experience of birthing a child, I'd forgotten all the bad bits of being a rep and, as I was equally clueless about my future, I decided to head back for a second season in Malia.

My confidence had grown and I had got really good at selling, and this made me feel like I had some sort of purpose in life. I made a decision that summer I would continue to go back to Club 18–30, and work up the ranks till I became a manager. And in 2009 that finally happened.

However, deep down while I loved escaping real life because it felt so hard, I knew it wasn't a lifestyle that I could sustain forever and it wasn't a career for life if I fancied having a functioning liver in my thirties. I had this desire in me to be successful, whatever that meant. My school and university friends at this point had gone into grown up careers and become teachers, lawyers, optometrists, doctors, managers and so on. I felt like I had somehow failed at the 'adult life' thing because I just didn't feel like any of that was meant for me. And yet, I didn't know what actually was. I had spent five years of my life living around the summer, getting odd jobs in the winter, making a great living in my eyes, but everyone kept telling me that I needed to think about 'real life' – whatever that meant.

I'm pretty sure that neither of my parents envisaged that, after spending over £100,000 on education, I'd be walking around the streets of Ibiza without footwear on, working for a company that basically helps 18-to-30-year-olds get pissed on holiday. I can tell you right now to this very day as a 35-year-old, my dad still thinks I worked as a family holiday rep for Thomas Cook. Sorry Dad – forgot to send you the memo! So there I was at 24, with a degree that I scraped through, five devastating heartbreaks, shit-faced and shoeless thinking: 'What the fuck do I do with my life?'

2

'Mummy, It's in Your Hands!'

Fast-forward a decade. As I lay in bed, thoughts were rushing through my head after I'd had a profoundly beautiful conversation with my agent Jessica about this very book, which until these words came out of my head and into physical manifestation, was just an idea.

All incredible things start as ideas – that's the beauty of life and the core of everything I teach. I had spent weeks putting my ideas on paper for this book to give to my publisher and I couldn't help feel the sense of resistance inside me. 'Why?' I asked myself. They were great book ideas, but it occurred to me that somewhere between the first excited call with my editor about the 7 billion new ideas I had, and actually putting pen to paper – I had somehow lost my way.

I was stuck in a metaphorical tunnel trying to find the light, and the more I pushed forward, ironically, the more I fell back. You see, pushing forward is way 'too human', and way 'too Ego'. While the doing and the pushing can be ever so helpful, in this moment my Soul was yearning for surrender. It needed space to come forth and share the real message – the real purpose of this book.

As I talked to Jessica, I expressed my desire to take the reader on a deeper journey of self-discovery that built upon what I taught in my first book *Just F*cking Do It*. Since roaming the streets of Ibiza barefoot, I was now a mother to three children, married to the love of my life, had made over a million pounds, and was the author of a bestselling book. Even when I see that in black and white it blows my own mind. How do I help people put together all the random puzzle pieces of their life to construct a gorgeous, completed piece of art they can call their life?

I had been super clear that my message for my first book *Just F*cking Do It* needed to teach people how I'd gone from a dispirited, anxious human with no clue about what she could do with her life, to the person I had become. I knew *what* had changed my life, and I wanted to teach those concepts in a digestible way, but what I had learned was esoteric and, dare I say it, woo-woo. My worry was that some would give up by page three (and some people did) and, oh boy, they loved to leave a review letting me know that I was away with the fairies and that the minute I started talking about the Universe I'd lost any credibility with them.

Those people will never be the people who 'find themselves', and for the thousands of readers who loved the book and wanted more, to go deeper into the discovery of themselves, this book you are currently reading will be that helping hand.

Even since writing my first book, I've gone on a deeper journey, and the level of success in my life has catapulted because I live and breathe the concepts I teach. It's a cliché, but I was lost and now I'm found.

Let's take a moment to analyse that phrase.

'Find yourself'.

People leave relationships to find themselves, climb Mount Kilimanjaro to find themselves, and I chose to spend my twenties drowning myself in Jägerbombs and cocaine trying to 'find myself'. It's this weird abstract concept that insinuates we are lost in life and we do not have Google maps to guide us back.

I remember once frantically running around the house, late for the school run, children at the door ready and confused while I searched high and low for the car keys. As I uttered a million expletives under my breath, convinced Richard (my husband) had lost them, my daughter looked at me and said 'Mummy, they're in your hand!'

That moment of complete and utter realization – that you had never lost the keys and that they had been with you the whole fucking time while you were frantically pulling out sofa cushions – is like the moment you realize you don't ever need to find yourself.

The scary part is, way too many of us have lost our way to wherever we were told or believed we were meant to be going. A fictional place, an invisible yardstick, the 'there' that we believe means success. We may feel stuck, or lost in life, but actually we aren't lost. We just forgot to look in our hands because we are so busy running around like headless chickens, trying to keep up with the endless requests of life and blaming the world when we feel stressed. The answer has always been there.

3
The Vanilla Life

We were once children dreaming of flying to the moon, being ballerinas and being parents to random animals we had adopted after watching an advert on telly. Do you remember those days before Netflix when you actually had to watch through adverts and you would be offered the chance to adopt a polar bear in Siberia or a killer whale in Canada? And once you had begged your mother to agree, this polar bear had mysterious writing skills and was able to send you updates on how excellent its life was now you were paying £5 a month to adopt him? Those were simpler days.

As children we dreamed and we didn't question how the polar bear had learned how to write – we allowed our imaginations to run free and then, suddenly, life became palpably more serious and constrained. We are flung into the school system at four years old, get told when we can sit, stand, talk and play. We are taught a bucketload of information for the following 12 years, and our intelligence is judged based on the retention of that information. Our self-worth is linked to whether we managed to get on the netball team, or play the main part in the annual school play, or whether we get picked to be head girl, or achieve the grades to get into university. We are taught what is required to become upstanding members of society and are pushed towards careers that will provide the elusive security of the nine-to-five.

It's almost impossible as children to listen to what our Souls are saying, because we are so busy listening to the wise words of parents, teachers and society who tell us they have our best interests at heart. And they do, but they don't know any better than the discoveries they've made in their own experiences. We get told to get good grades, so we can get a good job, so we can have a good career and pay our good mortgage on our good house with our good partner and our good 2.4 kids. They will go to a good school and you will have a good life as long as you stay nice and comfortable, realistic and good. Good people abide by the rules and do what other good people do.

But…

Good isn't great.

Good isn't extraordinary.

Good isn't pushing the boundaries of your own potential.

Good is like vanilla, and I for one am way more of a 'peanut butter and Oreo cookies' type of gal.

When I look at my children, I don't just want them to have a good life and get by. I want them to have a great life that they are grateful for every day, and I want them to do something that brings them joy, not just money. I want them to experience the world, live life by their own rules and contribute to other humans in a positive way, however big or small. I do not want my children nor do I want you to settle for what everyone else is doing. I don't want vanilla for you. I want you to have your cake, with a side scoop of ice cream, and I want you to eat it all – guilt free.

I want this book to wake you up. To grab you gently by the shoulders, lovingly shake you and remind you that the answers you wanted and the key to changing your life has always been right in the palm of your hand. I want it to bring about a shift in your own consciousness; to awaken you to the sheer possibility of this one life you are currently living. A pivotal component of you waking up is recognizing how you became who you are, and that there is a part of that contributing to you sleepwalking through life, instead of truly living it. You need to break free from the herd of humanoids. What is a humanoid you ask? Well, your first wake-up call is coming.

PART ONE
The Purpose

4
Herd of Humanoids

What sounds a bit like haemorrhoids, but is way more painful? Humanoid!

I need to be frank, this word feels so appropriate for describing the majority of the population but comes with a trigger warning.

Definition of *humanoid* as per the official dictionary of Noor Hibbert:

> *Noun*: A human that could be mistaken for a robot.

Humanoids are people that wake up, do what they need to do, so they get what they need to get done, so they can plod through life without ever really realizing they haven't really felt happy for a decade. See, I told you it's more painful. I am a recovered humanoid and consider this book your rehab. As I started to dissect every ounce of our experiences on the planet, looking at the people around me, listening to my clients, I began to realize that somehow as a human race we had in fact got it so freaking wrong.

Humanoids have become so programmed to do what others do that they have flung their dreams and ability to think for themselves to the curb like an empty fag packet, and have unconsciously subscribed to the perspective that life is about 'settling' and sacrifice. Most humanoids are living life with the singular big goal of having enough pension saved, so that *one day* they may be free from the slavery of the nine-to-five, two-day weekend and 21 days of freedom a year – a.k.a. holiday days.

As humanoids, we feel caged by the invisible prison bars of society's expectations. We are told what feelings are okay to express and how we should act in accordance with social etiquette. Once I completely lost my shit when I heard my six-year-old was reprimanded for yawning in class. 'That's very rude!' her teacher told her. Yes, even bodily functions are expected to have their own set of rules and know when to show up in certain situations. We are told what body we should strive to have and programmed to believe what 'they' want us to. I don't know who 'they' are, but this anti-yawning committee is also the same 'they' who tell us what kind of life we should lead to be upstanding citizens. We believe this narrative because everyone else is doing it, so it *should* be right. We get so disconnected from our own purpose, because our purpose, our *modus operandi*, seems to be *to do what everyone else does*.

Purpose tends to get all muddled up and confused with vocation – i.e. the thing that fuels your bank account and finances your human existence on this planet. Purpose in my eyes isn't really that at all. Yes, it's one part of it, but the purpose puzzle goes way deeper than figuring out what's going to put money into your bank account.

As I embarked into my late twenties and still felt at a loss as to what my purpose was, I became a curious observer of how humans go through life, as though I was visiting animals caged in the zoo.

Why were so many people depressed and why was suicide on the rise?

Why did more and more people need anxiety medication to get through the day?

Why was there a huge rise in unexplained chronic illnesses?

Why did an extraordinary amount of people feel 'stuck' and not have a clue how to move on?

Surely life wasn't designed to be a perpetual cycle of eat, sleep, shit, repeat and a myriad of rules and regulations that kept humans living in small invisible boxes?

I saw a crisis on our hands that went beyond the shitfaced and shoeless members of our community. I just knew we were meant for more and I wanted to understand why we had got so off course.

5
Red Lights

Imagine for a second that you have somewhere really amazing to go. You get in a car to drive and you get stuck behind a red light. But, the red light just won't change. You can see all the cars around you whizzing past and you have this awful feeling that you are going to be extraordinarily late or, even worse, totally miss the amazing thing you are so excited about. That's how most people spend their entire lives – stuck behind the red light that won't change with a deep knowing that there is somewhere better to go, with no clue when it is going to change nor daring to put their foot on the pedal when they realize the traffic light is faulty. Or even worse, they don't even ever think that there is anywhere better to go – standing behind the red light has become their de facto mode.

This leads to uncomfortable feelings that could be described as 'being stuck' – feelings of overwhelm, frustration, stress, numbness and even anger. These emotions have a negative effect on your body as your adrenal gland slowly drips cortisol, the stress hormone, into your body, like a leaky tap. When we deny our Soul the opportunity to drive freely down that highway and create the life we want, that perpetual red light frustration and anger manifests in a plethora of things – from mental health issues to physical ailments and chronic illness. It is not new information and has been scientifically proven time and time again, that stress leads to health problems.

The worse thing is, most people aren't even aware that they are creating a breeding space for illness inside their body as this slow drip of cortisol weakens their immune system. Most people are living in survival mode, not creation mode – they are living at an unconscious low-level state of stress, which means their body is out of balance.

There are different types of stressors, such as physical stress, chemical stress and emotional stress, and these all affect the homeostasis (balance) of our bodies. Our bodies can only deal with short-term stress – the primitive 'fight or flight' system which is inbuilt in us. This sympathetic response is great for short-term problems. For example, if a bear casually bowls into Tesco supermarket for a bag of custard doughnuts, our body gets us to run. But long-term stress is a one-way highway to disease, because no organism can tolerate it. What's interesting to note is that Western medicine has always purported that the mind and body are separate, which is why we have separate doctors to deal with mental health issues and physical body issues. When we start to see the body as a whole, as in Eastern medicine, we can start to truly grasp the damaging effects of mental stress on the physical body.

Chronic stress alters the immune system response and suppresses the digestive system, the reproductive system and growth processes. Our Souls are designed to grow, and when our minds stop that growth, it can have disastrous effects.

This is why leading a life that has purpose is crucial to not only your sanity but your vitality and physical wellbeing. Purpose in life can be conceptualized as having goals, a sense of direction, and a feeling that there is meaning to present and past life. For me, my purpose revealed itself over a duration of years. I started to free myself from my own mental 'stuckness' and watched, like a surprised observer, as my life completely transformed.

I decided to build upon my Psychology degree and did two postgraduate courses in Business and Executive Coaching, followed by Coaching Psychology. I trained as a strategic intervention coach, a rapid transformational therapist and an emotional freedom technique practitioner. All of this has helped me live my purpose of helping others create mental freedom, which as a by-product leads to physical freedom. If I was a superhero, my superpower would be helping people see through their own BS and supporting them by creating their own future.

Studies have shown that having a purpose in life has been associated with positive health outcomes among older adults, including fewer chronic conditions, less disability and longer life. I believe that a huge reason why we currently are facing a staggering increase in mental health issues and suicide is due to people feeling their life lacks purpose – because they have been so indoctrinated into the herd mentality of the humanoids.

Let me share some stats taken from Mental Health First Aid in England. They state that one in four people experience mental health issues each year, and that 792 million people are affected by mental health issues worldwide. At any given time, one in six working-age adults have symptoms associated with mental ill health, and mental illness is the second-largest source of burden of disease in England. Lastly, mental illnesses are more common, long-lasting and impactful than other health conditions, and these are the ones that have been reported.

I truly believe that a big problem is the discrepancy between what people dream their lives could be as children and teenagers, and the reality they are *actually* living as adults. Sometimes this is due to trauma and pain they experienced in the past that they feel unequipped to overcome, and so life ends up feeling so much harder. We aren't taught about our minds and how they work at school. We just know when we don't feel good and struggle to break past negative thought patterns.

Buddha said a characteristic of being a 'normal' human is suffering. When we are able to see that this state of being that we believe is normal is, in fact, completely the opposite and damaging, we can begin to transform and, as Hindus explain it, become enlightened. We simply cannot accept that life is about suffering.

But how can people live a life full of joy and full of purpose when we spend most of our lives worrying about how we will afford a house, and when we do, we worry about paying the mortgage and barely scraping by? The lucky ones among you may be able to take a nice holiday or three, but please, whatever you do, don't forget about saving for your pension! The whole goal of life is to save enough so when you do finally get your time back at 50–60, you can travel and have freedom. That's if your back hasn't given up on you. And of course if you start a family, forget about seeing them every day. You have two allocated days called a weekend. And 19–26 days holiday a year to do as you please in your OWN freaking life. We have got so used to this absolute insanity that we just get on with it.

That is why I've written this book. Because after my days in Ibiza, I ended up on a decade-long journey of life discovery where I began to unlearn this way of being that got me stuck in the first place. I transformed my life from a girl making £9 a sale, selling a weekend in Skegness to a bunch of boys from Coventry who would whip out their cocks at any given moment for a laugh, to someone with three beautiful children, a happy marriage and having created the abundance I dreamed of through helping others.

I became completely obsessed with understanding how to create a life that meant I never got stuck at red lights again. Don't get me wrong, I had fun dancing till the wee hours of the morning during my years abroad. Some of my most fun memories are from those years, and it taught me so many incredible skills that have served me so well as an entrepreneur, but I always knew it wasn't for life. *This was my one life and I wanted to make it count.*

6

A Reason for Being

As I sipped on my warm morning coffee with the Mexican sun enveloping my body and the smell of sea air lovingly swishing around my nostrils, I felt a sense of peace. Being by the Caribbean ocean, my toes dipped in powdery white sand, brought me an internal nirvana – I was feeling my *ikigai*.

Ikigai is a Japanese concept which simply means 'a reason for being'. This powerful concept refers to having a direction or purpose in life, that which makes one's life worthwhile. The misconception by Westerners who use the word *ikigai*, is that it's often wrongly thought that we should have only one *ikigai* that we must look for in life. This is incorrect and the Japanese use it in the plural form - yes, we can have many reasons for being.

Your *ikigai* doesn't need to be your vocation, and actually the word *ikigai* is almost never used to refer to something that is work-related in Japan. It's used mostly to refer to something that's very personal. For me, lying next to my two-year-old in bed with my face close to hers as I feel her warm breath on my cheek, is my *ikigai*.

Cuddling on the sofa listening to my kids laugh at a movie while chomping on popcorn is my *ikigai*.

Walking in the countryside wrapped up warm on a cold but sunny day listening to inspiring music is my *ikigai*.

Doing quiz nights with my family, and taking the piss out of my mum for getting all the answers wrong, is also my *ikigai*.

Those precious little moments that fill your Soul and make life worthwhile are your *ikigai*.

Humanoids have stopped focusing on their *ikigai* and are living a life driven by the external world, steeped in a fear mentality, glued to screens and disconnected from nature. This is the most basic level of consciousness, with most people trying to survive each day, and this has become the operating mode for life.

There is an innate worry that if we break out of the robot prison and try to create the life of our dreams that somehow something really bad will happen. This is because we have this incredible organ called a brain. And while our brain is very useful for storing data and helping us automate our daily processes, the job of the brain is to keep us safe, not happy. Like the air stewardess that gives you the side eye when you aren't paying attention to the safety demonstration because you are too busy scanning which of the 50 films you will spend your journey watching, it wants you to be on red alert for the risk all the time. Your brain will step in with a huge red stop sign when you are about to embark on something new. It craves the familiar, the comfortable and the secure. This is not conducive to breaking free to your bigger life.

Also, humanoids have a very limited perception of reality, one that could fit on the back of a postcard. One that is only limited by what the five senses can perceive, rather than what is beyond the capabilities of our human body. It's a perception based on the notion that 'we just do what others do because surely they are all doing it right?'

Wonderful as they are, our eyes clearly are not without certain limitations. We can no more see radio waves emanating from our electronic devices, than we can spot bacteria right under our nose. The visible light spectrum is the only segment of the electromagnetic spectrum that the human eyes can see, and that makes up one measly per cent. So if we can only perceive one teeny tiny per cent of light in front of us, then what the hell is happening in the other 99 per cent? To assume that what we conceive with our eyes is the truth of the world would be naive, but this is what humanoids believe. What I want you to start embodying is that seeing is *not* believing, but actually the complete opposite is true.

Humanoids can be wealthy, poor, black, white, brown, female, male, transgender and speak any language. And what you will find is that humanoids are everywhere you look, masked as lawyers, doctors, managers, shop assistants, air stewardesses, teachers, bus drivers and every other occupation. No occupation, race nor sexual orientation is exempt.

Some humanoids are completely happy being humanoids. They are so conditioned that they believe being a humanoid is exactly what they should be doing with their lives.

Some will never admit they want more from life because they can never see a way of getting it and don't care to change.

There are humanoids that are unhappy and want more and don't know how to get it.

There are the 'perfect on paper, not so perfect in real life' humans. The ones that do all the things they were *meant to do* to make them money and keep their good mortgages paid, but they feel a sense of numbness as they are devoid of joy.

They secretly want to whip off their corporate tie and step onto the stage of *Strictly Come Dancing*. But of course that's just a 'silly fantasy' and they quickly retreat to the humdrum of doing what needs to be done to get through another day. At least they have a glass of merlot as comfort and a good salary to soften the blow that they aren't actually happy.

Despite the fact that I really did not fit into the academic life of a private school and perpetually felt thicker than everyone else, I did actually end up with incredible GCSE and A level results. I got a 2:2 in my degree from a top university and, while I had no idea what I was going to do with it, this was meant to be my golden ticket to the perfect career. When you buy into that narrative – that education is your ticket to success – and it doesn't pan out like that, it leaves you questioning everything everyone ever told you about winning at life.

Perhaps you have found yourself, like I have done, staring at the clock, agonizingly watching the hands move round so you can welcome the end of the workday or week with open arms, wondering 'Is *this* it'?

Perhaps, like I did, you feel a knowingness that there is *more* to this experience we call life and yearn to unlock the gate to that *something more.* You are no longer willing to accept that you picked the short straw of the life journey. That *something more* can seem unclear, which leaves a sense of anonymous dissatisfaction with life. If only that *something* would stand up and make itself known so you can figure this shit out. Maybe you feel like you're on the cusp of something big, and yet don't know how to navigate your way to finding that.

Even after *all* the years of education, we aren't taught the basics of creating a life that fulfils us. We all know Henry VIII had six wives and what the fate of each of them was, but it seems that important mentorship on dreams, mindset, finance, life and responsibility got missed.

This epidemic of just 'existing' is a real one, and even if you are doing much better than just 'existing' and feel there is something way more you wish from your life, then I want you to know that you can change. You don't need to just exist.

What if we got it all backwards? What if life is not about going anywhere or becoming anything new? What if life is about *unbecoming* everything you were ever taught and remembering who you are? What if, like those keys in the palm of our hand, we are actually never lost and therefore never need to find ourselves? What if there was a way to reprogramme the software of our minds and be reset to factory settings – before all the bullshit the world taught us about life got installed?

Well, I happen to believe all the above to be true. Maybe it's about unbecoming everything that isn't *really* you, so that you can be who you were meant to be in the first place – someone who deserves to have everything they desire.

After many years of battling through life, I decided that none of what I was experiencing in my physical world made any logical sense to me.

None of it whatsoever.

And because it made no sense, this caused me a great deal of internal pain that led me to constant physical problems and ongoing mental health issues.

I'd like to invite you to see reality – but not as you know it. There are unseen forces available for you and tapping into them will help you co-create your life. Yes, you are the captain of your ship, me hearties!

Through this book we will look at those big ass questions that mind boggle and perplex the crap out of us. What is the point/meaning of our life as humans? What the heck is the Universe? Are we really able to attract what we want?

When we take a moment to make sense of these questions, I believe it creates a solid foundation for then moving toward your vision of what you want. If you want to preserve the 'eat sleep shit repeat' paradigm, then it's utterly pointless trying to live a life *on purpose* because it requires a level of awareness that you can transcend that belief. For you to at least understand that you have a choice, it requires you to remember who the heck you are.

You are not a humanoid my friend.

You are not limited, or unimportant, or too overweight to manifest your dreams.

You just forgot who you are. I'll give you a clue. Pure consciousness joy riding through this life in a human body.

We will delve into the world of living *ON purpose*. It's about choice, responsibility, executing presence and reclaiming your power by understanding what really matters to you and, therefore, learning that you can, in fact, live a life on your own terms. When we live *on purpose*, we intentionally choose more joy, recognize we have more choices, create more happiness and bring fulfilment into our lives. We stop the groundhog day in its tracks and become aware of how we make each second, minute, day, week, month and year count.

In Part 3 we will look deeper at your own unique purpose and footprint in this world. How do you make a difference to other humans? How can you contribute to waking others up? What beautiful piece of gene magic has gotten intertwined in your DNA that is your gift? And before you throw this book to the ground while hailing 'I don't have a gift, I'm not special!', I need to remind you to take a breath and to understand that this is one of the biggest lies we believe. That we aren't enough. What a load of big hairy bollocks. You don't need to find yourself, because you aren't lost. You just forgot. You got amnesia as your Soul splattered onto earth and incorporated into your physical body.

I've been hopeless. I've felt lost. I've wondered how I was so alone and whether life is meant to be so hard. I'm actually grateful for those times, because when we go through the dark night of our Souls, we awaken with a sense of possibility that trumps those dark moments – if we allow the light to come through.

Through the words in this book, my aspiration is for you to gain a new perspective. For you to deepen your connection with yourself and the field of infinite possibilities, and for you to wake up and realize that your life is for the taking and for the making.

Maybe there's another level of life you wish to reach, a 2.0 version of yourself waiting to be claimed and dreams that are lurking in the corridors of your mind, patiently waiting for you to bring them to fruition.

Life is not meant to be hard and, in order to break from the herd of humanoids, you'd better be ready to elevate your thinking to a whole new level.

So what's the trick? It's to become aware of who you *truly* are. Let's get this party started.

7
Who the Fuck Am I?

'The purpose of life for man is growth, just as the purpose of life
for trees and plants is growth.'

Wallace D. Wattles

*What is the actual point of the 80 or 90 years (or even 100 if you are
lucky enough) on this home we call Earth?*
Who am I?
Where am I?
What am I actually doing here?

It is indeed an incredibly risky business trying to answer some
of the biggest questions that one can possibly ask in the duration
of a lifetime. Many try to answer the question of what the meaning of life is, and they feel a deep existential void. A void that some
people try to fill with sex, drugs and rock and roll. Or in my case,
constant failed relationships, class As and Pendulum raves.

And the reason this question is so huge, and takes quite a brave
person to attempt to answer it, is because – if we are totally frank –
we will never ever *really* know the answer.

No one sat down with the Creator over a hot cuppa and tentatively asked, 'Come on love, fill me in – was there really a Big
Bang? Did Adam stitch Eve up? And how the heck did you manage to whip this world up in seven days?' while intently listening
and chomping on a jammy dodger as the Creator spills the beans
on life's greatest questions.

It's a question that culture after culture, religions and philoso-
phers have tried to answer for millennia, and each has created their
own interpretation. But ultimately, once again, this is probably the
most unanswerable question that there is.

So what do you do when you want an answer to one of life's most unfathomable queries? Well, you Wikipedia that shit!

Wikipedia is the foundation of all knowledge, alongside Dr Google, who will for sure let you know how many days you have left to live after you type in 'red rash on left knee' (the answer is almost always that you are going to die, which leaves you running for the NHS 111 phone line before you realize that you've accidentally smeared nail polish on said kneecap).

It's kinda fun to see what Wiki thinks the meaning of life is – and feels like surely the next best thing to a cuppa with the Creator. When I type in 'meaning of life', it pulls up the most popular answers. The following list is by no means exhaustive – we also need to take into account that there is also an unpopular list located on another website saved only for relegated answers, most probably on the dark web. I picked out a few of the answers, so here we go. According to Wiki, our purpose is:

- To realize our potential and ideals – which essentially means to chase our dreams
- To become the person you always wanted to be
- To matter: to count, to stand for something, to have made some difference that you lived at all
- To achieve biological perfection and to simply replicate and reproduce
- To seek wisdom and knowledge to tame the mind, and to avoid suffering caused by ignorance and find happiness
- To resolve the imbalance of the mind by understanding the nature of reality
- To leave the world a better place than we found it (we've massively effed up on that one) and take every chance to help another while on our journey here
- To contribute to the wellbeing and spirit of others
- To worship God and enter heaven in the afterlife
- To love, to feel, to enjoy the act of living – to simply have fun or enjoy life

- To seek pleasure and avoid pain
- To eat, drink and be merry
- To seek authority and power
- Religions suggest that our purpose here is to love something bigger, greater, and beyond ourselves, something we did not create or have the power to create, something intangible and made holy by our very belief in it
- Life has absolutely no meaning at all, because human existence occurred out of a random chance in nature, and anything that exists by chance has no intended purpose
- The answer to the meaning of life is too profound to be known and understood and you will never live your life fully if you are always looking for the meaning of life – so give up now.

As you can see, there's a whole spectrum of answers from people across the globe who have attempted to solve this mystery. What I am going to share with you is the interpretation that feels the best to me and I hope will feel really good to you – the interpretation that has helped me change my life.

It never quite resonated with me that we all inhabit Mother Earth for no apparent reason other than just to pay taxes and die. I don't buy in to the fact we are an accident either. Even as a young girl I had this huge sense that there was *more to life than what I was seeing*. This uncomfortable feeling that resided in me, leading me to question the strange behaviours of the human race.

I happen to believe we are here for a multitude of reasons included in the list of most popular answers above. I believe we are here:

- To find and live our most joyful life
- To learn to love ourselves and others
- To make the world a better place and contribute positively to humanity

- To help our Souls become wiser
- To remember how powerful we are.

Because there is no definitive answer, you get to choose. Yes, you get to choose what you believe the purpose of your life is and you get to live your life based on that purpose.

Just don't forget to eat, drink and be really fucking merry.

8

One in 400 Trillion

Are you ready for a truthbomb?

Whatever you choose to believe is your purpose, you need to know one thing. You, my friend, are a miracle. A full-blown, statistical freaking miracle. The fact you were born is an event so unlikely as to be almost impossible.

Scientists estimate that the probability of *you* being born is about one in 400 trillion. In order for *you* to be born, out of the 7 billion people on this planet that could possibly meet each other, your two exact parents needed to meet. We could go crazy here and note that in order for your exact parents to even exist, we need to take into account that your exact grandparents and great grandparents also needed to get jiggy with it (sorry for that visual!), otherwise your parents would be different people, and then their child may have been similar to you, but not quite you. So, if even one of your grandfather's sperm met a different egg, you would not be sitting here reading this book with your mind right now filled with the horrifying images of your parents and grandparents making sweet sweet love. Ok, sorry, I'll stop.

Now let's move away from the complexity of your lineage and thoughts of your grandfather's sperm and back to your parents even meeting. Not only do they need to be in the same place at the same time, your parents need to actually converse. I remember the first time I talked to Richard (my hubby), I had really been enlisted to be my friend's wingwoman. I had, 24 hours prior, just come out of a long-term relationship and was incredibly happy to be single and vowed to make the most of my time left on the White Isle. I had zero interest for the first time in my life in being in a relationship and was more than happy to assist my mate in getting laid. Never in a million years did I think that the drunk Yorkshireman who I was standing at that bar with, who annoyingly kept pinching my bum, would end up being the father of my three kids. To be honest it was a miracle alone that I could even understand a word he said without subtitles, due to his broad northern accent that my little London ears weren't accustomed to!

Back to your parents. So after they first meet, preferably your parents need to meet again before deciding to bring a human into the world. Then we need to take in the probability that the meetings turn into any sort of relationship that lasts long enough to result in them reproducing new humans. I read somewhere that the probability of your parents' chance meeting resulting in children is about one in 2000.

Now let's get to the probability of *you* even being born. Your parents need to get it on during the six days a month a woman is fertile. Then, on the proviso that your dad's sperm can survive the completely inhospitable environment of your mum's cervix *and* has the strength to swim all the way to the egg (go dad!) – it needs to make it all the way up the uterus. Did you know that when sperm enters a woman's uterus it triggers an immune response?! And that once sperm enters, the number of white blood cells increases, and they begin to attack the dying sperm?! You see, it's not an easy job trying to make *you*.

Next, your dad's sperm needs to break through a group of cells and penetrate the egg, otherwise it's game over. Once it meets the egg, the nuclei from the egg and sperm merge and share their genetic material. If all this goes to plan, the egg now contains all the genetic material it will need to become *you*.

Beautiful, unique, miraculous, one-of-a-kind *you*.

As you can see, being conceived is quite the journey, and if any of those steps don't go exactly right, your mother may never have even gotten pregnant with you. So what are the odds of your being born? Well, the probability of you existing at all comes out to 1 in $10^{2,685,000}$ – that's a 10 followed by 2,685,000 zeroes! By that definition of a miracle that I gave you at the start, I think it's safe to say that you are a miracle. So don't you think it's time to act like one?

9

Divine Homelessness

Having grown up in a semi-religious household, religion was rammed down my throat. I say semi, because my dad was a Muslim and my mum subscribed to her own level of Islam where she said if bacon was crispy enough, it didn't count as pork anymore and so therefore was okay. You get the conflict.

My mum believed in God but didn't believe that you needed to partake in all the rules that determined how good a Muslim you are. I think you should do whatever makes you feel good, but religion just never ever sat right with me and, because it didn't, I decided to become a very proud atheist in complete unconscious rebellion of my parents. I didn't want to say 'I don't know what I believe', so I was a clear-cut 'no freaking way'.

I decided that there couldn't be a God because there were starving children, murderers and wars. I couldn't believe there was a man in the sky with a long beard, who made the world in seven days and was judging me throughout my whole life, ready for when I died and went for Judgment Day. It all felt fantastically far out, and if God had all these rules about how to live life, the free spirit in me wasn't interested.

I felt disconnected from the notion that there was someone that we needed to bow down to, and so it was easier for me to not think about the whole concept at all. So I completely rejected it. I would cringe every time the word God was mentioned and would avoid all the religious ceremonies at school by telling them my parents were Muslim and didn't want me going to church. This was, of course, a load of bollocks. I just found a loophole in school whereby you could watch telly with all the real Jewish, Hindu and Muslim girls, while the rest of the school endured two hours sitting in a cramped chapel singing 'all things bright and beautiful' and praying to a God I didn't even believe in. I thought I might as well milk the fact I had Middle Eastern parents for once in my life, and this meant I could hang out with my best friend at school who was *actually* Jewish.

But as I grew up, I secretly started to feel something in me – a sense of knowingness that there was 'something' bigger than me.

Something bigger than us all.

Something that made every planet spin with precision, kept hundreds of species of trees growing, my body breathing and the world moving around the sun.

Something that controlled day to night and orchestrated every season with perfection.

Something that made the moon glimmer, the sun shine and turned eggs into chickens and acorns into oak trees.

Some level of intelligence that made tides turn, tomato seeds change into tomatoes, and that had perfectly designed the female body to grow and birth a baby.

This was not a fucking accident.

This was the work of a genius.

The sheer level of intelligence that is required to manage the tapestry of this whole magnificent Earth and everything that lives on it, is quite simply mind blowing.

I was kinda ready to start opening up a conversation around it all. But not in my early twenties – I was too busy downing neat shots of vodka and snorting coke off questionable toilet seats for that level of conversation, not to mention I was still trying to fit in – so it was best to park any deep, existential conversations till I was older.

It wasn't till I was 28 years old that a man called Dillon Dhanecha, philanthropist and coach, accidentally landed in my life. I say accidentally, but nothing in life is ever an accident. I love the saying 'when the student is ready, the teacher appears', and in my case my teacher was an incredibly wise man, who swore possibly even more than me. I signed up for a 21-day course he offered, not realizing at all that this would be the gateway drug for me into understanding spirituality from a completely different perspective. For the first time during my time on this planet, I was willing to listen, and what he had to say changed the whole trajectory of my life.

My secret suspicions were right, there is SOMETHING bigger. That *something* is divine. Some people call it God, some people call it Allah, some call it Mother Nature, and I will interchangeably refer to it as the Universe, Creative Intelligence and Source. You can even just call it 'something bigger' – it doesn't matter. Simply the recognition that something *way more* intelligent than us humans is running the gig will suffice. This thing hasn't got form, certainly isn't male or female and isn't the slightest bit judgmental. Phew.

I started to see that through my complete separation from this 'something bigger', I had become Divinely Homeless. Divine Homelessness is the state of being that encompasses a feeling that perhaps 'something is missing' in life, a knowingness that there is 'something more', a feeling of being 'stuck' and being completely disconnected from the intelligence that created us.

I had set up camp on the street corners of life, instead of residing in a beautifully designed home in the countryside that brought me joy. And while the word 'divine' has religious connotations, I do not see it in that way. Simply put, being divinely homeless means a separation from the non-physical, non-tangible, pretty-freaking-powerful thing that created everything, which also is incidentally part of you.

We each have a physical body which we can see in the mirror, and a non-physical part of us, not visible to the human eye. Both are made of energy distinguished by the different levels of frequency they vibrate at. The Law of Vibration states that everything in the Universe moves and vibrates at one speed or another. *Nothing rests.*

The things we can see with our physical eyes vibrate at a slower rate which is why they are visible to us. Your frequency differs from other things in the Universe, and that's why we think we are separated from those other things, when in fact we just cannot see that the 'nothing' between us is not nothing at all. It is energy we cannot see, connecting everything on Earth together.

The same atoms that make up plants, chairs and even this book, make up our physical body. Besides the frequency of vibration, the major thing that separates us from a book or chair is the non-physical life force making *us alive;* **the invisible energy that runs through us** that distinguishes us from inorganic matter. I will interchangeably refer to this life force as *consciousness* or *spirit.*

This life force gives us the capacity for growth, our ability to reproduce, keeps our blood pumping, our hair growing, and all the other continual changes before we die. The life force is the fuel that helps cells regenerate, and provides oxygen to our organs without us ever having to think about it.

The physical part is the part that most humans spend their life agonizing over. The wonky nose, the spotty skin, the love handles and ingrown toenails. Most of us don't take the time to even acknowledge the non-physical part of us as we go through life, which causes the disconnection and divine homelessness I speak of. Because we cannot see that part of us, we often do not realize it is ever present and ever powerful. That consciousness has unlimited pure potential waiting to manifest. This is eternal, infinite consciousness, free from all attachments, birthless and deathless.

This consciousness runs through each and every one of us, every animal, every plant. We are all connected because our consciousness is actually all part of the same source of energy that created this world. The Law of Oneness states that *we are all one,* and that we are all ONE with whatever created us.

Imagine that we are all part of one big Ocean of Consciousness and that we get poured into different buckets. Some buckets are big, some are small, some are red and some are blue. Some have broken handles and some are dented. And when the time is right the water gets poured back into the ocean and becomes whole again. Perhaps there was a Big Bang after all? A bang that caused the Ocean of Consciousness to fill billions of buckets for a certain amount of time. Out of the Oneness you were created as an individual. A Oneness from which all life comes, and to which all life returns.

We are all made of the same consciousness living in different buckets.

So yes, you are energy and you are connected to the Universe, but what happens is, as we become more and more human with every year we live on this planet, our connection to this Source becomes weaker. Like a really shit WiFi connection, it doesn't matter how many times you move to get closer to the router, you just can't seem to get what you want out of life. Every time you seem to catch a break, it's taken away and this happens because you haven't got a stable, strong connection. You can never disconnect completely, but the more Divinely Homeless you are, the weaker the connection, because you are living life purely through the lens that you are a human living in a physical world. In a small fucking bucket.

I am not religious at all, nor will I ever be, however I began to see that there is absolutely a manual to living life, and the rules were buried deep in the wisdom of books that have been around for hundreds of years. With this new understanding of who I truly was, the playing field of my life radically changed. Despite my aversion to religion, I began to find out that some of these religious texts had some of the big answers all along. Despite all the years of being a devout and proud atheist, and swerving anything 'spiritual', I started to see things through a very different lens and that's when my life began to profoundly change. I had this underlying feeling that I had been lied to all my life and I was ready to seek out the truth.

10

Anybody Out There?

'If anybody is out there, help me,' I pleaded. I was sitting in my car outside my daughter's nursery, looking up at the sky (that's years of conditioning right there!) and with tears streaming down my face.

I don't really know what I expected to happen after my cry of desperation from the carpark. There was no bolt of lightning that zapped me into a different dimension where suddenly I had my shit together and everything I wanted appeared out of thin air. Nothing actually happened. But as you will start to see as we go through this book, *something* incredibly profound did *actually happen*. My sheer desire in that moment flipped an energetic switch and catalysed a series of synchronicities that would lead me to this very moment. While that call for help sounded like a desire, deep down I'd reached breaking point and, without realizing, I'd made a decision in that moment. A decision that I no longer accepted my life as it was. A decision to change my reality.

After almost a decade of trying to understand how to make my one life count, in 2015, I became addicted to personal development. I was glued to reading books and listening to audios by the likes of Jim Rohn and Wayne Dyer, who became my new favourite people to hang out with. Everything started to make complete sense. Jim gave me motivation and hope. Wayne confirmed everything that I had ever questioned about our purpose – that we are here for a reason and we are not just skin and bones, designed for living a painfully ordinary life.

The plague of the human is we expect everything to happen immediately. We are continually bombarded with marketing messages that appease our human need for immediate gratification, and so we have become lazy. Why work out to get healthy if you

YOU ONLY LIVE ONCE

can take a magic pill and lose weight while chomping on a pizza? Why go out and buy things at a shop when you can click a button and hours later the item is at your door? Why build a business that is scalable when you can make money online and become an overnight millionaire with this new fancy social media company? The problem is most of this messaging is bogus, but as humans we like easy, quick and comfortable. When it comes to changing our lives, while it can be relatively quick to understand the real rules of life, applying them may not be so easy because it requires you to change your whole paradigm that has been yours for decades. Your paradigm is your perception of life, based on the beliefs you created from childhood.

The most fundamental concept that I want to impart to you is this: *we are way more powerful than we will ever give ourselves credit for.*

So, who am I?

I started to understand that I am, and you are, pure consciousness living a human existence. That in fact we are not separate from what created us, but are part of a large tapestry of universal creative intelligence. The non-physical part of us is pure potential waiting to be actualized: we have been designed with all the faculties necessary to grow into the most abundant version of ourselves. Our job is to undo the messy web of human beliefs and to get back to that potential. Yes, being a human has stunted our growth.

I've come to understand that what I can actually see with my eyes is a fraction of what is happening around me at any given time. I've come to learn that thoughts are misunderstood and have become like a cancer to humans. Instead of being used to create our lives, they have evolved to being our masters destroying our dreams.

I started to become aware that it was my Divine Homelessness that was the problem and that navigating back to my rightful home was my only choice to feel happy.

What I soon learned is that purpose is layered, complex and ever evolving. It's not one destination, but a beautiful journey of your own evolution. Getting back to connection with the non-physical part of us and thus reclaiming the power that we already had.

Life shouldn't be designed to set us up to fail – or to *just survive*. Surely whatever created us didn't want its creations to suffer? Because that was exactly what I kept seeing - people suffering.

Suffering is elusive and can look like a millionaire celebrity in Hampstead Heath on the glossy front cover of *Cosmopolitan*, who secretly drinks a bottle of wine every night to mask the pain of her childhood trauma. Suffering can be seen in the girl on the Peckham council estate who was abused as a child and relives it every day, so she numbs with cocaine. Sometimes the suffering is a child experiencing the divorce of their parents, or it could be the post-traumatic stress of a veteran serving in the war in Iraq. The world was shocked that Prince Harry had been suffering, trapped within a system that stopped him ever fulfilling his unique purpose. No one seems to be exempt and the spectrum is wide. Pain is caused by something physical – but when we are suffering, it's in the non-physical part of us.

The scariest thing is many people don't even realize they are suffering. They have become such high-functioning sufferers they are used to it, and we are part of a huge system that has not been designed to help us thrive.

Take a moment to think about this. Think about your life, the people around you, and ask yourself: How many people do you know that are truly living their best lives on their own terms?

Is this a common sight or are those the anomalies, the lucky ones?

Shouldn't we all have a chance to live *our* own lives how we want?

The quality of our life is determined by the quality of the questions we ask and it's time to start questioning everything.

II

There Ain't No Solid, Baby

If you were to ask people if they live in a solid, physical world, most would without hesitation reply, 'Of course, don't be silly!"

But what if I told you that was incorrect?

The scale of the illusion of our very own lives is mind-blowing.

What if I told you that every morning when you wake your solid body up, from your solid bed, take a shower in your solid bathroom, eat your solid granola and yoghurt, with your solid children who are being exceptionally annoying that morning, and then do the school run in your solid car to the solid school – that none of it is *actually solid*? Say what?! Yes, my darling, life is not what it appears to be.

The idea that we aren't solid took over me. The first point that needs clearing up is the idea that matter and energy are distinctly different like chalk and cheese. What we perceive to be solid matter, quantum physicists have now said is an illusion to our naked eye and that we aren't solid at all. Quantum physics claims that 99.9999999 per cent of what is called 'ordinary matter' is, in fact, empty space. This is because science now knows that both the electrons that spin in the energy field located around the nucleus and the nucleus itself are made up of nothing more than oscillating energy grids.

And wait for this kicker – all the space that you see in between objects is actually not 'nothing' but is bursting with energy that our human eyes cannot perceive. Solid matter, in the strictest sense of the word, does not exist! Rather, atomic structure is composed of oscillating energy grids surrounded by other energy grids, which orbit at ridiculously high speeds. We are taught that our material world is made up of solid atoms and that everything physical is solid as a result of this. But hold your horses, atoms have no solidity, so how can they create a solid world? As illusions in the world go, I don't think there is anything more extreme than me breaking this to you – there ain't no solid baby. This sounds so fabulously fantastical and sci-fi that your brain may be trying to find an ounce of logic in it, so you can make sense of what I am saying. But some things are just beyond our human comprehension.

As I explained in an earlier chapter, humans are made up of energy, not solid matter! In fact we are made up of approximately 7 octillion atoms, all vibrating at an incredible speed. Rub your hands together right now, really fast, for 30 seconds. Close your eyes and feel the sensation after. That is the feeling of your not-so-solid atoms vibrating – that's the energy you are created from and you can feel it.

I remember thinking, back in 2015 after being presented with this information, 'Wait, if I am not physical and am in fact "nothing", then why can't I walk through walls?' I always wanted to do that as a child! If you are holding this book in your hands, why isn't it just slipping through your fingers like it would for Casper the ghost? That is because everything is vibrating at different frequencies. And there's electromagnetic resistance between the different frequencies. So my body is an electromagnetic field of information and the wall is an electromagnetic field of information. The bump I feel when I attempt to walk through the wall is the connection and resistance between these electromagnetic fields. We can see physical things that vibrate at a lower frequency and we cannot see things that are vibrating at a higher frequency.

Enter Einstein: 'Concerning matter, we have been all wrong. What we have called matter is really energy, whose vibration has been lowered as to be perceivable to the senses. There is no matter. There is only light and sound.'

Whenever we hear or see anything, we don't actually hear or see unless that information is decoded by the brain. Our eyes and ears are simply instruments for decoding that information. The vibrational information fields that are generated by the vocal chords when your partner nags at you are decoded by your brain via your ears; that's the only reason you can hear them. Cut off your ears and there will be no nagging partner in your reality anymore! Do not try this one at home!

The same applies to your eyes. The light hits your eyes and your brain then decodes the light wave information that results in what you're seeing in front of you. Without your senses decoding the 'physical' world you see, you would be in complete blackness with no sounds, no sight, no smell, no taste and not touching anything.

As you can see, quantum physics is a pest to mainstream science, because it causes us to question everything we have ever been told about our life as we know it. Nikola Tesla so wisely said: 'The day science begins to study non-physical phenomena, it will make more progress in a decade than in all the previous centuries of our existence.'

Most of us are taught traditional mainstream science at school, which has provided lots of incredible teachings, but our whole lives are governed by the premise that we are merely solid humans living in a solid world. Medicine, government, education and media bases everything we do on this huge illusion – which I for one have begun to see as the definition of insanity.

12
One Body, Two Selves

We are all one consciousness having different human experiences.
For you and I, our experience right now is that of a human. Unless somehow you are a polar bear reading this book. In which case I'm glad I've started reaching a new audience!

Each of us are made up of two parts or selves; our physical and non-physical. As we discussed previously, there is a part you can see and a part you cannot. Imagine that before you were born, the non-physical part of yourself was flying through time and space like a bird, and then you decided to take some time from all the freedom of flying about and see what it's like to live a human life inside your bucket. When we are born as a human, we forget that we were once not a human flying through space. Your non-physical self is that part that has joined the physical at birth, giving you the human experience.

That non-physical part of you is part of the Universe, part of that big ocean. I will interchangeably refer to non-physical part of you as the Spiritual or Higher Self.

Your Spiritual Self has a non-physical mind, infinite wisdom and a Soul. Our physical self is created through our human experience – let's call this self our Ego. Please note that this reference to Ego should not be confused with Freud's definition of the Ego in traditional Psychology. Your mind also has two levels: the conscious and the subconscious. Your mind is *not just your brain*. I like to view the conscious mind as part of the physical part of you, your brain. I like to view the subconscious as part of the non-physical part of you. Your conscious mind can accept, reject and originate thought. Your subconscious mind can only accept what is impressed on it by the conscious mind. We will dive deeper into this later as we delve into the power of your paradigm.

The non-physical part of you not only has an intellect, but it has a Soul – which I personally like to see as the heart of your Spiritual Self. Your Soul provides the unique energetic blueprint that gives you your unique personality traits. The 'nature' part of you, not the nurture. The Soul isn't an organ and cannot be dissected and investigated by scientists. It holds all the knowledge, wisdom and love that you have got from all your lives. Yes, I said *lives* and I'll share why I have come to believe this theory later.

Your Soul has work to do on this planet during this lifetime. Many cultures believe that before you are born, you sign an invisible soul contract that determines what you are meant to do during your human lifetime. Your Soul is here to guide you to living your best life. It knows that you are powerful and connected to the creative field of possibilities.

Your Higher Self is the *real* you, the consciousness that is so, so much more than the physical form you believe is you. Your higher self is your greatest teacher and gives you nudges, also called intuition. Intuition, when broken down, simply means tuition from the inside, wisdom from the Soul.

The core assumption of your Spiritual Self is that you are perfectly safe and secure as you are. This part of you has a knowingness that you live in a world of abundance and you do not need to look for happiness outside of you. It understands there is plenty to go around, and that when you gain, so does everyone else. The inner wisdom of your Soul urges you to follow your heart and it nudges you from the inside out. It doesn't bother with justification because it expects you to know and embody it as Truth. If you attempt to debate with it, it will merely give you the same answer again and again. Your Truth is a pervasive knowing inside of you. It urges you toward expressing yourself through things that bring you joy. The Spiritual Self is the identity of the non-physical part of you.

Now I'd like to introduce you properly to your good friend Ego. Your Ego is your social identity constructed by your brain through your human experiences. This is the persona your mind creates so that it's able to joy ride in this human body for 80, 90, 100 years, if you are lucky. It is your social self, created by the stories and experiences of your life that helps you to navigate this human world. When we go about days saying 'I', we are embodying that human identity – the Ego. Your Ego is created based on your experiences of the past. Whatever you identified with as you grew up has created the identity of this Self. It could be your gender, race, religion, material possessions, nationality or profession. It also identifies with different roles such as mum, dad, daughter, son. And, really importantly, it decides what it likes and dislikes, forms opinions on things and creates a defined sense of self based on all experiences and knowledge from the past. This is why the Ego can also be referred to as the Story Self.

Think about how you decided to become who you are at this very moment. You heard words which are just sounds that have meaning. When we hear those sounds as children, they create the labels and identity of the 'I'. Words are made up of just five sounds that the brain decodes through the ears.

As Eckhart Tolle so wisely writes, 'Do you believe some combination of such basic sounds could ever explain who you are, or the ultimate purpose of the universe?'

The answer is no, and this is why the Ego is limited by nature. The underlying assumption of the Ego is that the world is unsafe. The Ego assumes you live in a world of scarcity, which means you must compete to live the good life. In the eyes of the Ego, the world is composed of winners and losers, rich and poor, successful and unsuccessful; a world of division far, far away from that big Ocean of Consciousness.

The Ego's focus on life is from the outside in. It reacts to external stimuli and must have external results to feel good. 'I will be happy when I have money, success and the house of my dreams' is the mantra of the Ego. The Ego tends to equate having more with being more, so the more handbags, watches and shoes I have, the more I am as a person.

The voice of the Ego comes from your head. It needs to justify itself to you through logic and will engage you in a mental debate to prove that it's right. The Ego thinks it runs the show and the noise of the Ego is loud, like a two-year-old throwing a tantrum. In essence, your Ego is the part of your identity that is rooted in fear and made as a result of the human experience.

When we can bring the Spiritual Self and Ego together in alignment, we can create harmony and restore balance in our minds and life. Unfortunately, no one handed us the manual for this, so for the most part we live life through the lens of the Ego and the external physical human world, and remain disconnected to the non-physical spiritual part of us. We stay rooted in fear and Divine Homelessness. Conversely, living life just through the Soul can keep us in an airy fairy place where things don't manifest. You need Spirit and Ego to work cohesively – you need the non-physical part of you and the physical part of you to partner up like best buddies on the road trip called life.

When we return home, we come back to the recognition that we have a non-physical part of us that is connected to the *something* that is way bigger than us. But our huge disconnection to this reality is what has caused way too many of us to feel lost, stuck, overwhelmed and unhappy. The constant need to GO somewhere in life, to be better than others rather than just *be*. We have become a species of human doings instead of human beings. Ego likes to Do. Spirit likes to Be.

Therefore, I like to put forward the notion that our purpose is to understand and connect with this spiritual, non-physical part of us that is connected to the Universe Intelligence. And with that power comes great responsibility. Cue the lightsabers.

You have a mind.

You live in a physical body.

But who are you?

You are a powerful spiritual being with unlimited potential living a human existence, and it's time to shine baby.

13
How to Win at Life

Imagine life as a video game. There are infinite levels of possibilities that you can rise to. Whether you reach those levels depends on how much you *decide* to grow, but not externally – the growth must happen internally. Growth is a decision. The more you grow internally, the more levels become available.

I used to love that moment when playing the Nintendo when you would direct Mario to eat the mushroom that turned him into a larger version of himself and suddenly he had all this power – well that's what needs to happen to you. Note, Mario doesn't rub the mushroom on his body, he ingests the mushroom which causes him to grow. The growth must happen from the inside out.

When you become a larger and better version of yourself, when you upgrade your paradigm of the world as you know it, you can have the ability to transcend through the levels, collect the stars and make your way to the flag at the end. When we accept that we are not just physical beings, living in a solid world, we can move past our limited thinking that what we see in our physical world is the only truth.

In school, we don't get taught how to beat the baddies (the narrative of the Ego), how to collect the mushrooms that make us bigger (connect with our consciousness and pure potential) or to find special stars that give us superpowers (use our thoughts to create rather than react). Yes, we are taught how to grow up and move towards a career to pay the inevitable mortgages, but it's not the common narrative that we can all become truly abundant in all areas of our lives and that is what we should strive for. That *needs* to be the new narrative for the sake of our Souls, and our children.

Changing the narrative and stories involves a level of thinking that goes far beyond the thinking of most people in your life. This breaking free can result in all sorts of magical shit happening, but can result in you losing people along the way. Whatever happens, you need to know that the only person keeping you tied to the limited version of yourself, *is you*.

That's what I believe is the *whole point of life*. Our purpose is to see the invisible handcuffs that have been limiting us and find the courage to take them off. The emphasis needs to be on courage, because change can feel like standing on the edge of a cliff looking 1000ft down. The handcuffs have been put on by you and can be removed by you at any time. You just need to take the key and take them off. However, the handcuffs are comfy, the handcuffs are familiar, the handcuffs have been a part of your life for so many years that it's actually kinda scary to take them off, to break loose and feel the freedom. We have identified with the handcuffs as being part of who we are. All the other humanoids are wearing their handcuffs so you don't want to be the odd one out.

'Just look at us. Everything is backwards, everything is upside down. Doctors destroy health, lawyers destroy justice, psychiatrists destroy minds, scientists destroy truth, major media destroys information, religions destroy spirituality and governments destroy freedom.'

Michael Ellner

This quote really hit a chord with me when I read it. I felt triggered by it. Whilst I think it's a huge sweeping generalization, there was undeniable truth in this. I was triggered because it highlighted so much of what I'd felt was so wrong, that we indeed as a human race had made some momentous fuck-ups that were causing disastrous effects.

If your perspective is, 'Well, that's the way it is', then you my friend got off at the wrong train stop in life and you will be stranded in no man's land till you leave your physical body. I decided to get back on the train, leave the humanoids behind and start finding my actual home – my Truth. I wanted to thrive in all areas of life, explore all four corners of this beautiful globe, spend precious time with my children as they grew up, and be able to make a bigger impact on the world.

Don't be the person that falls asleep on the train and misses their stop.

Don't be the person that gets off at the wrong stop and doesn't see the board that shows all the other trains going to other destinations.

Get back on that fucking train to wherever you need to go to find the joy in your life.

You didn't pull the short straw, you are not unlucky, you are not destined for an average life. If you can learn the rules you finally have a chance to win.

That surely is our number one purpose?

The whole freaking point?

To live a life of joy and abundance?

You don't need to go through life thinking that you need to catch a break, or that you can't be happy till you have achieved X, Y or Z.

We have forgotten our whole purpose is to *enjoy life*, to savour the beauty of our planet, to come together in collaboration instead of competition. To spend time with your families instead of worrying about the next like on Instagram. To stand up for what you believe in. To be real and authentic instead of polishing our pixels and adding filters to every photo to keep up the illusion that we are perfect. Your whole purpose on this planet isn't to just survive another day and make sure you are keeping up with the Joneses. Surely not.

The fact you are sitting reading this is a choice you made to take action for your life and I'd like to guide you through that. We are all part of one quantum field, that huge ocean connected by invisible energetic cords. We are all connected, so I don't believe it's a coincidence that we are here together.

You were meant to read this.

This may sound crazy but truly, if your way of thinking has got you to where you are today, but you aren't entirely happy with how your life is – then it's time for you to be open to a new perspective.

The perspective shift is that your one and only purpose is to live a life of your own design.

'How do I make it happen?' I hear you say?

Well, my dear, I thought you'd never ask...

PART TWO

On Purpose

14

Hacking the Spiritual Algorithm

'Nothing splendid has ever been achieved except by those who dared believe that something inside them was superior to circumstance.'

Bruce Barton

I remember the first time I heard the theory that we are all living in one big simulation. My tiny ears pricked up because, of course, I have been using the video game analogy for years to explain life to people.

I found it fascinating that many physicists, cosmologists and technologists will happily entertain the somewhat radical idea that we are all living inside a gigantic computer simulation, experiencing something similar to the *Matrix*-style virtual world that we think is real.

When this theory was posed to me, my instincts rebelled because, just like when I was forced to believe in a religion that didn't sit right with me, this idea felt so far-fetched. Surely Nick Bostrom (who wrote the 2003 book *Are You Living in a Computer Simulation?*) was smoking crack when he came up with it. Our lives feel so real. *How could it be a simulation? But then again, we aren't even solid. What the fuck is going on?*

I'll never forget being 11 years old and experiencing the roller coaster simulator at the Science Museum. As I boarded the little airplane-like craft with about ten others and buckled my seatbelt, I had no clue what I was in for. After 30 seconds, I realized why people had been screaming on the last ride and was regretting my decision to come. I was close to crying before my friend said, 'Cover your eyes silly!' As I put my hands over my eyes, suddenly

I was just rocking gently and the fear left my body. I spent the rest of the day ruminating how real this virtual reality had felt.

Not only had this question about the Universe being a simulation perplexed me, I had read so much and seen endless proof that the Universe has been designed with precise mathematical order displaying repeating symbols and signs, such as the Fibonacci sequences. If the very world we lived in was a simulation, I started to wonder whether the Universe is made of some sort of code. I began to research this and I discovered that it isn't such a far-fetched idea and is supported by many great minds. But what does that mean for us as humans? Well, that we need to question the very fabric of our reality, and that if we can learn how to hack the algorithm of the Universe, we can then win at life.

I know what I've just said has the capacity to be quite the mindfuck, and remember that cognitive dissonance will kick in whenever we entertain something that is so out of our mental comfort zone, but there's enough evidence to at least make you *question reality*.

I personally don't spend too much time trying to make sense of it because, just as we never get answers from the Creator on the deepest darkest secrets of the world, I don't think we will in this lifetime get definitive answers on the above. But what I hope to do here is to show you that what you see in your life may certainly *not* be what you have previously understood to be truth. The nature of reality is *not* something that is set in stone and agreed by all scientists and mathematicians across the world. There's still a great deal of stuff that is beyond the comprehension of the human brain.

That's why when I teach you about manifestation and your instinct says, 'Really?!', that you need to truly believe that there is stuff that logically you will never grasp. I am here to encourage you to open your mind to that. You don't need to understand the how, the what and the why, just be open to the knowledge that no one knows anything *for sure*, so the somewhat far-fetched idea that humans can create their reality with their minds is something that is still very plausible. In fact, it only takes a quick Google search to reveal that scientists and Nobel Prize winners actually know very little about how the brain works, and this is one of the greatest challenges of neuroscience.

So, how do we hack the spiritual algorithm to transform any area of our life? There's a five-step method that I've developed over the years and I would like to share this formula with you. It's something I work with my clients to embody and implement inside my coaching programmes.

Introducing my Manifesting Method. This system has worked for me time and time again, and also for my clients across the globe. People have manifested their homes, new babies, more money, better health and career promotions. Most importantly when you start to implement this, you become the most aligned joyful version of yourself. This creates a really great connection to the Universe, which also then guides you so much more effort-lessly to your own purpose.

Step 1. Decide what you truly want and activate in the fourth dimension.
This is goal-setting on steroids. Truly figuring out what you want, why you want it and how it's going to make you feel – are the three essential ingredients for manifesting anything.

Step 2. Uncover the beliefs you have in regard to your desire.
Annoyingly, as humans we are plagued with saying 'but' after most things we declare we want.

- I want to find a husband, *but* he doesn't exist
- I want more money, *but* I am stuck in my job
- I want to cure myself of cancer, *but* the doctors told me it's not possible.

We love to but-but-but-freaking-but all over our dreams. How-ever 'buts' are great as they are indicative of our limited thoughts and programmed paradigm. When we can bring them into aware-ness, they don't have the same stronghold over us and we are able to challenge them. Limiting beliefs keep us stuck in a life that is, well, limited. We are the results of what we saw, heard and experienced as children, which gave you a warped view of the world as a result of the projection of your parents' own fears.

Step 3. Reprogramme your mind and create an identity designed for success.

This is a big one. Our personality creates our personal reality. We believe that our identity is carved in stone, which it isn't. If you don't believe you can get to level 10 on the videogame, then you will stay stuck at level one. The great news is, we can be whoever we want to be thanks to neuroplasticity. Creating new beliefs that create new thoughts, that drive new actions will change our results.

We need to create new beliefs and make sure they get accepted into the subconscious through repetition. Our subconscious is what is energetically attracting or repelling our desires, so we need to change the seeds that are growing into the fruits of our life.

Step 4. Tune into Universe FM. Every. Freaking. Day.

This step isn't linear – it's a way of life. It's a choice to be conscious about your thoughts and energy on a daily basis so you are firmly rooted in the vortex! This is a conscious choice to show up as the version of you who sees life is out to support you rather than be against you. The you who leads with love, not Ego. The you that chooses to be a better fucking person.

Step 5. Take inspired and guided action in the physical world.

This is the step where most go wrong because of misguided books on manifestation that make it seem like magic and that it requires nothing from you but to visualize. I hate to be the bearer of bad news, but this is completely incorrect and sitting on your arse eating Oreos and catching up on the *Friends* boxset will not result in a million pounds falling out of the sky and into your lap.

Back to the video game analogy I used earlier. Imagine if I said, 'Here's a video game of your life and, in order to get better at life and collect the most gold stars, you need to conquer each level.' Imagine if I then handed you the console to win at the game but you never picked it up. You would be stuck at the starting line, timer ticking down and the games console would overheat because you left it sitting there for days on end – never touching the damn thing.

You need to pick up the console and actually do the work! You need to use your console (your body) to partake in the game of your life. You need to use your physical body to make shit happen!

The greatest thing is, unlike a video game where I mostly have no freaking clue what I am doing, the guidance for winning the game of life is installed right into your hardware – yes, you have an inbuilt Success Mechanism. You are designed to succeed. You will be guided to take action through sprinkles of inspiration, lightbulb ideas and gut feelings that seem to come out of nowhere. This guided inspiration will lead you through a series of incidents that will eventually result in your achieving your fullest potential.

Hacking the spiritual algorithm is not hard, but takes practice and commitment to master the steps, but as you do, watch how everything in your physical reality begins to morph into something better than your dreams.

15

Tell Me What You Want, What You Really, Really Want

The famous Spice Girls song whirled around my head on repeat as I sat down to map out what my ideal life would look like – *for the very first time in my life*. Surely it would make total sense that if we have only one life with limited time – the one thing that we don't get back – that we should at least choose and design how we wish to spend each day, week, month and year?!

Surely that makes complete and utter sense?!

In fact it's staggering, when I ask people if they have ever sat down to think about what they really want out of their life, how many say no. Most people are living life like it's an accident. According to the good ole dictionary, an 'accident' is anything that happens suddenly or by chance without an apparent cause. Antonyms of 'accident' include purpose and preparation. To live *on purpose*, by definition means to prepare and have an intention or objective.

Studies have time and time again shown that people who set goals in their lives are likely to be more successful, yet the amount of people that intentionally create their lives is tiny and we need to question why. Living *on purpose* means becoming intentionally aware of how you spend each day, each week, each month and each year – no more goddamn Groundhog Day. And this does not just mean what you are doing in the external world, this is a choice of how you are feeling internally.

We simply aren't taught to go within and feel into what we would like to do. We don't get encouraged from a young age to choose and create and design our lives. No, no, good little human-oids feel powerless to this.

The greatest challenge to us in consciously creating is that we are born into a system – a system that, without us ever really knowing or questioning, coerces us into what we *should* do with our lives. The system does this gently and over time. This isn't a pepper spray attack down the alleyway where the system runs off with your bag, never to be seen again. This is a slow attack on our Soul from the minute we get flung into school at the tender age of four.

Schools are amazing for many reasons and, while I had a tumultuous experience in my school years, my kids love their school. They teach kids how to read, write, socialize and give us parents a few minutes to grab a cuppa without being asked for the fifteenth time in an hour, 'Can I have a snack?!'

But what is school *really* doing to us? It's teaching children how to be good little humans who do what other humans do. It teaches us how to conform to societal norms, behave in accordance with our culture, and sets us up to go off and get a job with most likely capped income and a limited amount of free days to do what you choose in life. And the majority of us will accept this without ever really questioning it.

Just take a moment to think about what I've just said, because when I started to *really* think about this it became evidently clear that I had been caged and tamed my whole life, groomed to fit into a world that didn't really have my best interests at heart. I don't want my children to be bound by arbitrary rules of how we should construct our life.

It got me to thinking about a shoe-related incident with my daughter.

'Mummy my shoes feel funny!' Mimi said to me with her face screwed up in frustration. She was only two years old and had put her shoes on the wrong way.

'You have them on the wrong feet my darling, that's why they feel uncomfortable.'

'No mummy, they are right!' She screamed in my face in righteous protest.

Fighting with a two-year-old who believes they are right is always risky, but trying to convince her that her shoes are on the wrong feet and trying to convince people they are living life on autopilot, and that they are meant for more, felt distinctly similar.

We are walking around with our shoes on the wrong feet wondering why we feel uncomfortable. But if you dare to tell a human they have got it wrong, many will defend till they go blue in the face that their shoes are on their right feet, just because they look at everyone else wearing shoes on the wrong feet. We will fight for what is wrong, just because others are doing the same.

I began to ponder all the aspects of my life that I didn't like.

How much of this life was actually consciously chosen by me?

How much of what I believe was I conditioned to believe?

What did I *really* want to do with my life?

Who was I before I became what everyone else wanted me to be?

Why was I walking around with my shoes on the wrong feet, uncomfortably hobbling my way through life?

Many of us don't really know what we truly want because we have been doing what we have done for so many years, that it's like someone has smothered us with lidocaine and we have become numb. We get so wrapped up in being 'sensible' and getting 'comfortable' that we deny our longings because it's the responsible thing to do.

If there were no if's or but's, what would you desire? If you had no fear, what would you want to achieve? Think about the desires you have hidden in the dark corners of your soul because they were too crazy or cringey.

Step One of the Manifesting Method is deciding what you want. Decision is different energetically than a hope or a wish. It has power, it has faith. Decision says I'm doing this, not I'm hoping to do this. Sometimes we don't always know fully what that is, so starting with what you do *not* like about your life gives you an opportunity to map out what you do.

Starting with *not this* provides the gateway to *this*.

16
Not This!

I resented getting up for work when it was dark on a winter's day. It felt cruel having to leave the warmth of my duvet for another day cooped up in an office with people who made me feel utterly uncomfortable. Starting the day by dreading the day surely could not be the answer to living one's best life.

I didn't like the fact that the weekend was my only time off with my friends and family. Who invented this? Probably the same people that decided that yawning is rude! How were they even hired for the said job of allocation of days for humans to abide by? Can you imagine the job advert for that: 'Seeking innovative people to allocate days of the week so that humans know when to work and when to have fun. Pay negotiable.'

It felt wrong that I had to ask permission from another human, who felt they were way more superior than me, if I could go on holiday. Not to mention the fact that there were only a limited number of days in the year that this was even allowed, and you needed to fight the rest of the workplace to get them.

I despised having to explain and justify why I needed time off to look after my child if they were unwell. Being a mother is a full-time job that no one pays you for and it did not sit right with me that anyone would have to feel bad about taking care of their own children.

I couldn't stand the fact that, when I was pregnant and suffering with morning sickness and unbelievable tiredness, I would need to work eight hours a day, especially given the first 12 weeks of pregnancy are so vital and most miscarriages happen during this time. I feel there should be a law against this. Maybe I should run for Parliament and put this one through!

Those were just a few of the things that didn't sit right with me about the 'real world'.

I wanted to escape. I wanted to feel free.

All the above situations stopped me feeling good, and when we don't feel good, we vibrate at a lower level and we stop attracting what we desire as per the Law of Attraction. I am and always have been a free spirit, a globetrotter, a lover of sunshine and appreciator of mojitos – preferably lovingly sipped while toes are dipped in soft white sand. Which is why I found all these rules really hard to stomach.

Even when I first set up my business and got freedom for myself, I was then bound by my husband's job which is why I made it my mission to earn enough so he could quit. It wasn't enough that I became uncaged, I needed him to be as well!

I wanted to live life by my rules, have more time to have coffees with my friends, to travel the world on my own accord, to be with my children, and the chance to make enough money to never worry.

I also wanted to live in a world where wars didn't happen, racism didn't exist, terrorists didn't want to blow up buildings, our planet wasn't dying because we treated it so badly, and adults never hurt or abused children. This was going to be harder to crack, but starting with my own happiness had to be the first step to ever being able to make a wider difference.

Fighting for power and money seemed to be the thread that ran across the globe, and I didn't like it one bit. There is a dark side to being human that I found very hard to stomach. How had humans somehow collectively gone off course and how was the madness of existing like this somehow perceived as sanity? I wanted to be part of the change, but I had to start small and work my way up and that meant first figuring out how I created freedom for myself, before everyone else.

So let's start here. Grab a piece of paper and divide it into two columns. One side I want you to write down everything you don't like about your life. Get specific. Don't just write, 'I don't like my job'. Write why you don't like it – is it the role or is it the boss? Is it the hours or is it the location? Think about all aspects of your life from money to career, to health and body. Think about your relationships, friendships and social life. Do this right now.

In the second column, I want you to write what the opposite of what you don't like would look like. For example, if you don't like your weight at 12 stone, the opposite would be your ideal weight.

Now you have flipped your *not this* to your *this*. You now have some sort of roadmap to help guide you to a better way of living.

Next, I want you to write how it would FEEL to be living the opposite in your life. That is all we do as humans, we search for things and work towards goals because they will make us feel a certain way. We mistakenly think we won't feel better until we have the Mulberry handbag, the job promotion, the life partner or the size 8 body. Most people think that money would make them happy, but if you were to be given ten million pounds but you were locked in the basement of your house forever, would you feel happy? Of course not, because money is just the vehicle to give you experiences that **induce a feeling.**

But shouldn't we just be grateful for what we have got instead of focusing on what we don't?

Gratitude is a powerful purveyor of desires and we can be utterly grateful for what we have now and still not be completely satisfied. In fact dissatisfaction is a perfect state for creation! One of my favourite mantras is *Grateful, but not satisfied.* Dissatisfaction is a powerful vehicle for helping us move toward what we want, because as humans we are built to grow. There is never a finish line in life. There are limitless levels in the video game, which is why you can always unapologetically strive for more, if you fully embrace the journey with joy. When we focus on the fact that we don't feel good rather than accepting and being grateful for the very moment, we stay locked in a negative state, where we forfeit our present happiness for the future we desire. This was something I learned years after being locked in the said negative state.

Previously, I explained that I think uncovering your own unique purpose is a journey of peeling back the layers. In order to get closer to the answer of what your unique purpose on this planet is, answering the question of what the meaning of life is and what is the actual point of even being a human full stop is important. It is completely ridiculous to be looking for your own unique purpose if, ultimately, you think that the reason you're here is by accident.

When you realize that your life is for the taking, to love, to grow, to contribute to others on this planet, you understand that living life on autopilot is simply not an option. When you embody this philosophy, not only logically but in your body, it's the time to take life by the balls and start making every day count. That may feel like some cliché quote on an Instagram post, but it's the truth.

Doesn't it make complete sense that, once you understand that you were here for a bigger purpose than just procreating and existing, and that once you start understanding that your job here is to remember how powerful you are, the most logical next step is to start really making every single day of your miracle life count!?

When I was working in a sales job, after many failed attempts of starting a business while on maternity leave with my eldest Layla, who is almost 9, I hated it. I woke up every morning with a low-level sense of dread, already counting down the hours until I would be back home. This is exactly how *not* to live *on purpose*. I wasn't in a position to leave that job, so I couldn't change the external circumstances at that moment in time, but what I did have control over was my state of being and attitude each day showing up to it. That's how one lives *on purpose*. We recognize that we can choose our attitude and we have complete control over how we perceive a situation.

In the words of the incredible Austrian psychologist Viktor Frankl: '*Everything can be taken from a man but one thing: the last of the human freedoms – to choose one's attitude in any given set of circum-stances, to choose one's own way.*'

When you become deliberate about how you choose to view every situation, you are making a conscious decision how to spend your precious time on this planet, even if the situation isn't your ideal. By doing this, you raise your vibration by bringing in more joy and therefore as a by-product you are the perfect magnet for attracting your desires. This is what I call Tuning Into Universe FM. And while it may feel completely out of your reach that you could leave your job, build a side hustle, attract the soulmate, lose weight or create any freedom and more income, I need you to know that is *simply not true*.

As humans we experience something called cognitive dissonance. The term cognitive dissonance is used to describe the mental discomfort that comes from holding two conflicting beliefs, values or attitudes. As humans, we desire consistency in our attitudes and perception, so any conflict causes feelings of unease or discomfort. If you told a caveman that it's possible to land on the moon, he would tell you that's crazy. Tell someone in 2021 that it's *not possible*, then they would also tell you it's crazy.

When I tell someone that I make more money than a doctor and lawyer put together and I didn't slog at uni for seven years, that creates cognitive dissonance for them. I'll never forget sitting in this accountant's office as a 31-year-old who had done her second six-figure year. I could feel her eyes scanning me in my cheap leggings and hoodie and her brain trying to make sense of the numbers she was seeing. 'How have you made all this money?' she inquired.

She wasn't intending to be rude at all, but I could feel the cognitive dissonance seeping out her pores. 'I manifested it all – the Universe is my BFF!' I chuckled away. I always love throwing that at people because I can almost see their logical brain spontaneously combust!

We as humans, know an incomprehensibly small amount about what's possible for us, as I've already outlined thus far in this book, and while designing a life on your terms may feel uncomfortable right now, I can assure you it's all very possible.

When you are tuned in and tap into that universal field of possibilities, through consciously choosing to live *on purpose*, your unique purpose will unveil itself like a burlesque dancer seductively moving on the stage of the Moulin Rouge – it will captivate you. But you won't be ready for this unless you are spiritually and energetically available for the next level of your life to make itself known to you. You need to have your arms wide open to receive more abundance.

Personal boundaries are also so important because they set the basic guidelines of how you want to be treated in your life. Every time you say yes to everyone else when you don't want to, it means you are saying no to yourself. Read that again. You then become energetically drained and could end up resentful. It is not selfish to put yourself first.

Most people feel the need to please people because they are operating from an unconscious childhood belief that they need to be liked and validated. If creating a life that fills you with joy requires you to create better boundaries then that is exactly what you need to do. This will force you to look at what you truly value in life and then take an unapologetic stand for that.

Getting clear on what and who you no longer accept in your life is the first place for creating change. Living *on purpose* requires you to be painfully honest with yourself, more honest than you ever have been. It means saying no to anything that doesn't bring you joy or help your life progress.

17
What Truly Matters?

When someone asks me what truly matters to me, the lyrics from George Michael's song 'Freedom... freedom... freedom...' whirl around my head. Freedom is one of my biggest values in life. Alongside love, family, friendships, travel, impact and spirituality.

What does the word 'value' mean to you? Can you define it?

Simply put, values are what you believe matter most in life and values differ among people. They are the driving force behind your actions. As children we are taught values such as kindness, as teenagers we are taught the value of education, and as adults we are taught to value security. But most of us are leading our lives driven by the values *imposed on us* by those we grew up with rather than given the opportunity to carve them out ourselves.

As you venture into the delightful realm of mapping and creating your ideal *on purpose* life, it's crucial you decide what *really matters* to you. When you have values that guide your life, you can always use them as a yardstick for seeing where you have gone off course.

How can you expect to know what you want out of life if you don't know what you think is important in life? Knowing what you value gets you that much closer to an answer. If you value travel in your life but you only have 21 days a year to take holidays, then you have conflict about what is important to you and what is reality. This is what causes internal discomfort. If you need to make a decision about your next steps in life, your values can steer you toward the right answer.

Getting clarity on your values will help you declutter your life of things that you really do not want, need or believe are important.

This is true for people too. When you know what's important to your life, you become better at cutting out all the crap.

Having our values guide our day also means we are less likely to make emotional decisions. We can get stuck in negative feedback loops in the past, or be fearful of the future. However, if you can take a hot minute to ask yourself, 'What would someone who values X do right now?', then you just might find an answer that isn't charged with emotions.

On top of all these incredible reasons for why values matter, they help you develop a stronger sense of self which increases your own confidence. When you know what you stand for and what you don't, these provide the foundations for creating goals that actually matter – *Soul goals*.

You have been designed to succeed, baby, you just need to redesign your identity to align with the successful version of you.

When we are clear on what we don't like and tip it on its head so we know what we do, and when we know what we truly value, then we have a roadmap for creating our best life. Taking some time out of the hamster wheel of life to sit quietly and truly ask ourselves what we want is a gift that most of us never afford ourselves.

The first step on the path to succeeding in living a life *on purpose* and screaming *carpe diem* from the rooftops with joy, is knowing that we need a roadmap. We are designed for success, but we need to know where we are going. You cannot manifest something if you do not know what you want to manifest, which is why taking time to answer all the questions in this chapter is crucial. You cannot activate that incredible imagination of yours if you don't have anything to visualize.

> 'The faculty of imagination is the great spring of human activity, and the principal source of human improvement. Destroy this facility, and the condition of man will become as stationary as that of the brutes.'
>
> *Dugald Stewart*

As I've been saying the whole time, we aren't designed to fail, we are designed to succeed, and we just need to be restored to factory settings to a time before all the BS was programmed into us. In 1960, Dr Maxwell Maltz wrote his hugely successful book *Psycho-Cybernetics*. It altered the way psychologists, self-help authorities, athletic trainers and behavioural experts understand how the Success Mechanism in each of us works to achieve both large and small goals. This Success Mechanism relies on us focusing on the end result and desired outcome. We have been given something so incredible that other animals do not have – Creative Imagination – and we must use it. When Dr. Joe Dispenza talked about being greater than our circumstances, he was referring to us being able to use our mind and imagination to see a better version of our lives. When we get lost in our imagination, we have now transcended what is happening in our physical world.

You do not need to be focused on the *how* because that's what the creative field of possibilities orchestrates – focus on the end and the means will unveil themselves. More on that later. It's important to note, that those who stay focused on the *how* will interfere greatly in the fruition of their desire.

Right now all you need to do is focus on what you truly desire and establish that as a clear vision in your mind.

1 What would you like to do with your life? Think about what career you would be doing, where would you be living, how you would spend each day.

2 What hobbies would you pursue? Most of us put hobbies on the back burner because of lack of time and energy, but think about fun things that you would enjoy to take up.

3 What would your ideal lifestyle be like? For me, I like to have one week a month off and I like to go on holiday and adventures at least five times a year.

4 What specifically would you like to experience in your life? Think about this like a bucketlist of things you want to do, perhaps it's skydiving, or swimming with sharks or

eating a candlelit dinner in the Atlas Mountains. Whatever it is, write it down.

5 What things would you like to learn? Whether it's sailing, Spanish or sewing, get that down on your paper.

6 What would your ideal week, month and year be like? Describe it in detail.

7 Which of these things would you regret most not doing?

Now you have clarity on what you truly desire, it is time to uncover what could be stopping you from living your most *on purpose* life.

18

The Shitty Committee

When I was 14, I fell in love for the very first time.

It was the craziest emotional rush of just pure bliss and joy. I had dreamed about falling in love since I was about ten. Is that normal? I don't know, but after years of unrequited crushes, and even wrapping up my calculator to give to Frances in Year 3 in the hope he would be my playground husband, I finally met Izzy.

Izzy was good looking, funny and for some reason it was fashionable at the time to tuck your Adidas trousers into your socks and wear your cap at a 45-degree angle so it was kind of lifted off the top of your head. He was the *perfect boyfriend*. There's magic in that first relationship where you count every single hour together as a milestone. After one month of courting, he wrote me the most divine letter that covered two sides of A4 – my first love letter that outlined his excitement for our future, marriage and children. I still have it 20 years later. It came accompanied with a tape filled with a compilation of the greatest love songs of all time. Life was absolutely amazing, and it was the happiest I'd felt in a long time.

There is nothing quite like the first relationship you're in, but equally nothing quite like the burn of your first heartbreak, especially when you are being dumped for someone else. My four-month love affair ended abruptly by one text message delivered to my tiny Nokia 9310.

No one ever prepares you for the pain of your first rejection. I think I must have repressed some of the pain, or perhaps it just got replaced by the seven further heartbreaks I endured, but I can assure you of one thing, my mind went on a fucking field day after that.

Noor you are not good enough. You are ugly. You must be too fat. You aren't sexy. Your bum is too big. You will never be loveable. You should have had sex with him.

So, what has my first boyfriend got to do with anything? Well, everything. It exemplifies the power of our paradigms. Your paradigm consists of pre-installed limitations and the multitude of concepts fixed into the unconscious mind. These beliefs and concepts form your identity. Our experiences in the physical world will always reflect our identity. We will think thoughts that are in alignment to our paradigm and what we believe about ourselves. Shitty beliefs equal shitty thoughts. And we all know by now that shitty thoughts don't help us change our life, but yet many of us have them on repeat. So, in essence, your paradigm is a powerful invisible force that becomes the filter through which you perceive life and controls the outcomes. I had a glitch in my software and a belief I wasn't loveable – and my breakup from Izzy revealed it.

I had gone through a lot as a child. Having experienced six of the adverse experiences on the Adverse Childhood Experiences (ACEs) ranking, I was the poster girl for the kid who would most likely end up as an addict, homeless or jobless.

It all started to change at the age of four, when a girl came up to me in the school playground and told me I was ugly and pointed out my bushy eyebrows. That was the first time I started to realize I was one of the brownest people in the school and I looked a bit different to others. It was when I noticed that people always struggled with pronouncing my name and commented how unusual it was. I didn't like that feeling at all. I didn't want to be unusual or different.

At nine years old, my whole innocent world came crashing down when one of my closest friends told me they had been sexually abused by a family member. I was sworn to secrecy and kept this devastating news close to my chest for a decade. At 11, I was being bullied badly and dreaded every morning going to school. I had truly started to embody the belief there was something very wrong with me if someone felt the need to bully me. At 12 my parents started going through a divorce which ended up in a toxic battle of mind games and resulted in me becoming estranged from my father, who I started to believe did not want to fight for us. At 15 I experienced my first heartbreak by being dumped by my first 'love'. At 16 I was in a relationship with an older boy who emotionally and mentally abused me and then tried to commit suicide and told me it was my fault (and that if I ever left him, he would do it again).

I looked at the packet of Prozac in front of me. At this point, I was hoping the pills would give me some peace from my own mind and pain.

How had I got to this point after just a mere 16 years of doing this thing called life? It's not like *all* my thoughts were intruders, illegally squatting in the space between my ears, forming a committee with the sole purpose of making me feel that drinking the bottle of Malibu that was stashed under my bed was a good thing. I did have good thoughts and I did have happy times, but for the majority of my teens and then into my twenties, I was plagued with these bouts of depression and anxiety that immobilized me.

I'd find myself suddenly bursting into tears around the dinner table or curled up in bed listening to a repeat of sad songs while I allowed the Shitty Committee of thoughts to take over my days, my weeks and even my months. I would listen intently to everything the voices inside my head said as though they were the dictator of my life, and I was merely their slave. It felt as though once they got grip, it was hard to walk away. I had mastered the brave face, but internally I was at war with my mind.

By 16, the spark in me had started to fade, or probably it was beaten and sucked out of me as I began to realize that all the nursery rhymes we sang as children were warning us of the perils of the big wide world. Jack and Jill only wanted water, and Jack ended up smashing his head open. Humpty took a much needed bit of respite on a wall after an eggcellent day out and, despite all the efforts of all the King's soldiers, he couldn't be fixed. Don't get me started on the baby that was abandoned on the treetop by two completely idiotic parents. Where the fuck was social services? The baby fell. Of course he fell, he was placed on a treetop! Were our parents warning us all along that life was going to be a shit show?

The reason I was depressed was because my mind was stuck on a never-ending shitty playlist from the years prior. You could argue that I had a chemical imbalance in my brain, but no one checked the chemicals in my brain before handing me a pack of Prozac. To assume there is an imbalance is a risky business when handing out medication that has severe side-effects, including suicide. What I do agree was imbalanced was the stream of negative and helpless thinking that I was experiencing, in comparison to joyful moments of living in the present.

In my case, thinking had become the enemy as is unfortunately the case in so many. When I was anxious, it was the thoughts of the future that plagued me, sending my heart into a flurry of palpitations, causing my breath to quicken and nausea to settle in. It was the fear of the future and the voice inside my head assuming the worst for every situation in front of me causing me bursts of anxiety. If it wasn't my thoughts clinging onto the errors of my past, or the worries of the future, I would have been happy, but I'd become a prisoner of my own mind.

The problem with the ACEs is that it is limited and doesn't account for many of the traumas that a child can experience, and it really misses the mark for so many adults who are suffering. For example, I never was personally sexually abused, but I was so traumatized about finding out at the age of nine about sexual abuse that it resulted in me having nightmares for the following decade. Equally something that may not seem particularly traumatic to one person, may affect someone else deeply because of the context of their life.

For example, the relationships we have with our primary care givers as children has a profound effect on how we feel about ourselves as adults, and feeling unloved by a parent is a form of trauma for a child. My lovely dad would be the first to tell you that he was emotionally unavailable, and he was more angry with us than affectionate through our childhood. As a little girl all I wanted was my dad to love me and give me affection. I didn't know any different, but I distinctly remember being jealous when I saw my friends with loving dads. *Why did my dad not love me the same way?* He would always kiss us on our foreheads after we got tucked into bed, and I loved those moments, but I cannot remember much else than that.

Psychologist John Bowlby's Attachment Theory suggests that we will create an internal working model of our parents that we later internalize as our sense of self. This attachment correlates to how we then experience ourselves and how we are in relationships. So even after my breakup with Izzy, I took the belief I was unlovable through to all my following relationships, unconsciously realizing it was destroying the foundation of my future happiness.

By the time I was 16, I'd had enough! I had had enough of people trying to hurt me and enough of realizing the world wasn't a very nice place. And then to add to the mix, after being diagnosed with depression at 16 and anxiety at 19, I had in fact started to completely own the identity that I was a depressed and anxious person and the Shitty Committee would take permanent residence in my head. That was just the way it was and I would need to learn to live with it. This was who I was, because it was what the woman in the white coat said. And the Shitty Committee never failed to confirm this.

When I hit 19, I was introduced to drugs. I had been very, very anti-drugs till I was 19, but peer pressure is a real thing, people. The drugs catapulted me into a whole different world, but for every amazing night of being lost in the altered state of consciousness, the next day would bring the hardest comedown to real life. Taking cocaine, pills or MDMA, became the *modus operandi* for the weekend, and sometimes the whole week at university. I began to suffer with painful insomnia, heart palpitations and uncontrollable leg spasms. This was terrifying, and in those moments, I would worry about what damage I was doing to my brain if it was signalling my leg to involuntarily fling itself into the air with no warning, when all I was doing was lying in bed feeling sorry for myself.

The comedowns made my anxiety worse, and the bouts of depression felt even more palpable. But strangely it seemed worth it for those nights out where I lost myself in a high that I couldn't get from real life. I would punish myself mentally for being so dumb when I saw my swollen lip as a result of chewing it unconsciously whilst off my face, and swear I'd never do it again when I struggled to sleep for days. The drugs fuelled the Shitty Committee like kerosene fuels fire, so falling pregnant with Layla-Rose was the best thing that ever happened to my mind, body and soul.

I had dreamed of being a mother since my early teens, adoringly cooing over tiny footwear in every shoe shop. I'd endlessly daydream about holding a baby in my arms and celebrating Christmas with a brood of children running around. I realized as I grew older, my desire to have children was fuelled by the desire to find true love. I loved loving people and the bond between mother and child seemed like something so incredible.

Becoming a mother forced me to not drink or take drugs and, for the first time in a decade, I moved away from all that shit and started to focus on how I could better myself – I finally had a reason for living or, as the Japanese call it, my *ikigai*.

But just because I'd become a mother, the Shitty Committee didn't stop holding their board meetings. This time there was a new agenda, new minute notes and I was plagued with a whole new set of debilitating thoughts around motherhood, money, my future and my relationship with my then boyfriend Richard.

I had to give up my 'career' working for Club 18–30 and I hadn't actually grown up and got a proper job before being flung into motherhood, as I had always envisaged. My anxiety during pregnancy and the first years of my daughter's life reached a crazy high as I ended up taking a job for the sole purpose of making money and was subjected to working for a chauvinist male manager who seemed to enjoy making me feel crap at any given moment. I was trapped – if I left, I knew I'd never find another job as a pregnant woman. This feeling was all too familiar to many people that I had the pleasure of working with. This sense of being trapped in jobs and relationships with invisible handcuffs. No one is physically holding you there, but the Shitty Committee knows exactly what to conjure up to make you feel that way.

As I embarked on the journey of self-development and a quest to overcome my depression and anxiety without medicating myself, I began to learn crucial learnings about all the challenges I had been through as a child. The reason I was sad was because I had given negative meanings to everything that happened to me and believed all the thoughts that the Shitty Committee threw out because they confirmed the paradigm I had created as a child.

- I decided at four that I was different and would never fit in
- I decided at nine that I couldn't protect the people I loved, and they were harmed, and I couldn't stop it
- I decided at 11 that there must be something gravely wrong with me that someone would want to bully me
- At 12, I decided that my own dad didn't really love me.

At 15 I decided that, because I got dumped by my first boyfriend, I was unlovable and not good enough which confirmed the belief I had created as a result of my relationship with my own father. This formed the template for every relationship I had and I never understood why I was constantly anxious and fearful in relationships.

The meanings we give to these events create our thoughts about the events. As children we see life in black and white. We don't have the capacity to look past the very moment and see beyond what is happening to us. I had chosen to see those experiences as a reflection of me as a person.

Think about everything that has happened in your life and become aware of what meaning you gave it. What decision did you make at that time about **yourself?**

Most people I've met have had varying levels of experiences that have left a negative imprint on their heart and caused disruption to their present life. That is why I am so passionate about helping people find a way to heal from their past and make their life count despite their history.

The truth is, I couldn't protect anyone from being sexually abused at the age of nine. It was not my fault.

There was nothing wrong with me for the bully to make me their victim, that person was projecting their pain onto me.

My dad loves and loved me more than anything. He believed that taking a step back would spare us the pain of being caught between parents who were fighting, and he always knew that we would become closer and stronger than ever - which we did. What's important to understand is that our parents are also a *product of their conditioning and experiences as a child*. My dad lost his mum at 18 and it broke him. He was shipped off to boarding school in the UK by himself at ten, and that was utterly traumatic, not to mention the lack of support to deal with the grief of losing his mum so young. He didn't know how to show affection because he had been hurting for so long. Yes, daddy issues are a real thing and so are mummy issues. The relationship I have with my dad now is one I could have only dreamed of as a child, and he is one of my best friends and confidants, but that came after many years of both of us healing our own wounds.

My first boyfriend was a young boy who was guided by what his penis did. We were so young! That's not his fault - it was his hormones! Funnily enough, we caught up in our thirties and he shared how the memories of us are always something he treasures.

When we identify solely with the chatter of our mind, we become lost and Divinely Homeless. We get sucked into an abyss of overthinking, worrying about the future and analysing the past.

As children we put two and two together and get 'I am not enough' but, as an adult, we have the ability to reflect on our past and see it for what it was. You have and always will be enough.

Choose to give it a new meaning. Look for the goddamn silver lining, even if it's just a speck. Look at where you have got your wires crossed and made a wrong decision about who you are as a person. Look at where there is technicolour beyond the black and white.

If you want to change your life you need to change your paradigm. It doesn't matter how much you want to believe something on a conscious level, if you believe something else in your subconscious, then you will not be able to attain it. *We need to integrate belief and behaviour to transform every area of our life.* Since our subconscious paradigm is what is being projected on our world, we need to shift that paradigm. When we do this, we begin to change the energy of the electromagnetic field we are broadcasting.

Earlier I talked about the two levels of the mind – the conscious and the subconscious and how the body is an expression of my mind. Our collective purpose is to understand WHY we are the way we are and HOW we can change it so that we can all change our lives and then help raise the energy of the world as a whole. Right now billions of people on this planet are living life through the lens of a paradigm that has been created in childhood.

In order to multiply yourself to the highest level, you need to create division in your life. A division from your mind. You also need to recognize that paradigms are not fixed in stone and that through discipline and repetition, you can choose a new identity.

When we can create division from the mind, we realize that we are the thinker of the thoughts and that we also have the power to witness those thoughts; this alone shows us that we are separate from the thoughts.

This concept literally blew me away when I first heard it. It explains the countless arguments in my mind as though I had some sort of split personality. I was able to witness what I was thinking, so that alone meant that there were somehow two parts of me.

In every given moment we have a choice, a choice to witness the thought and shut it down. To look at the thought and challenge its very truth in our hearts. Is that thought TRUTH? Like 100 per cent cold hard facts?

You have the power and the choice to change everything when you choose a new thought.

19

You Are Not Your Thoughts

'You are a thinker of your thoughts, but they are not *your* thoughts.'
Say what?!

Those 13 words turned my life on its head.

When it comes to the transformation of humans, I have always been fascinated with how this happens on a psychological, spiritual and biological level and I started to realize that for all humans, our problems stem from how we *think*.

When most people think of the mind, they immediately envision the brain – which is an organ. The mind is not a thing and is no more a brain than your love handles are. The mind is an activity, the movement of dynamic thought energy and your greatest power when it comes to creating your future. However, it is grossly misunderstood and therefore we allow it to unconsciously work against us instead of for us.

We trust all the thoughts and that voice in our head as though *they are us and our truth*. After all, if we can hear it in *our* head, they *must* be our voice, right? Those thoughts must be the purveyors of entirely factual and correct information that we should diligently abide and live our lives by.

Big, fat, fucking wrong.

Our brain is an organ, like a big Google database, and every second of the day information is flowing in through these invisible antennae decoding the world and filing the information in there. Brain cells are activated by light waves, sound waves, taste, smell and touch which consequently affect the vibrations of the cells in our body, which also determines what we attract vibrationally as per the Law of Attraction.

As our brain deciphers information from the outside world (via our five senses) and runs it through the database, our brain turns that information into energy *that we can understand* - thought energy. That information literally becomes the thoughts we hear.

We interpret this plethora of thoughts as us *consciously thinking*, but the following distinction changed my life. This decoding of information is *not us creatively and consciously thinking*, **it is us reacting and responding to the outside world at every millisecond.** The thoughts are just a response to the information we are receiving through our five senses. We then respond to that incoming information and we believe we are thinking for ourselves.

You see, we think 60,000 to 70,000 thoughts in one day – and for most of us, 90 per cent of those thoughts tend to be the same as the day before. That's because most of us live day-to-day similarly to the day before. We execute the same routines as we wake up to a brand new day, having the same disputes with our stubborn toddlers, meeting up with the same work colleagues to undertake the same daily work tasks, to come home to the same partner to have the same conversation about how our very same day went. Sound familiar?! That's why our brain doesn't really need to think new thoughts.

We are simply going through life on autopilot and don't realize that we have the power to choose and create new thoughts. We forget that actually we aren't limited to the information that is *coming in* and that we have the ability to *push* information out. We can end up spending most of our lives reacting and responding, instead of using our thoughts to CREATE. This is how we miss out on truly using our imagination powerfully and cultivating thoughts for the greater good of our lives.

We become unconscious slaves to the external information coming in, frantically deciphering and responding, instead of taking a moment to use our mind to manufacture new thoughts that change our reality. When we change our thoughts, we change our feelings, which changes our behaviours and then consequently our results in the physical world.

There are three parts of the brain that I want you to know about when it comes to long-lasting transformation. The first is the **neocortex;** this is the thinking brain and the seat of conscious awareness. Your neocortex is plugged into the environment via your five senses. It is the theoretical, analytical, philosophical and intellectual part that loves to learn. When you learn something new, you create new circuits and synaptic connections in your brain. However, it is remembering and implementing the information that maintains those circuits and then eventually creates new behaviours. And don't forget: new behaviour equals new experiences and outcomes.

For example, as you read this book on uncovering your purpose in life, the information is being stored in the neocortex. Simply reading this is causing neurons to fire in your brain and synaptic connections to grow. But it's only if you take on board what this book teaches you, then make the smart decision to **apply the principles**, then you will start to see a long-lasting change. Simply *reading* this book won't create the long-lasting transformation that I know you desire. Putting those thoughts into action causes neurons to organize new networks that reinforce what your thinking brain (the neocortex) intellectually took away from reading this book. This will then create a new experience as you implement something new.

When those neurons form a new string that creates new thoughts, it then causes a new feeling or emotion. You see, our thoughts have a powerful and pervasive effect on our bodies. When you think a thought (or have a memory), a biochemical reaction begins in your brain causing it to release certain chemical signals which change the vibrations in our body. We as humans invented a word to describe this conscious awareness of the level of the vibration and chemicals in our body – a 'feeling'. Feelings or emotions are *energy-in-motion* at different frequencies. Emotions like joy, love and excitement vibrate at a high level and emotions like sadness, anger and jealousy vibrate at a lower level. That's why you may hear people refer to others as either 'high vibe' or 'low vibe'.

The moment you begin to feel these emotions as a result of that new thinking and new experience, you then activate the **limbic system of the brain**. The limbic system is **the part of the brain involved in our behavioural and emotional responses**. Now you are not only just thinking, you are feeling it and you are beginning to *embody* that new information. Your body is starting to learn what your mind has intellectually understood. This creates new feelings which cause you to take new actions. For example, you are reading about how to manifest (creates new thoughts), then you get excited about this (creates new feelings), and now you are then more likely to take the action to make it happen (creates new outcomes).

When the mind and body become one in this way, you activate the third part of your brain – **the cerebellum**. The cerebellum is the memory centre of your brain, where new habits are activated. This is where 95 per cent of your personality exists by the time you are 35, because who you are is a result of the habitual thoughts, attitudes and behaviours of your life. Our personality creates our personal reality: those habitual thoughts create the same feelings that drive our behaviours and create the results also known as our personal reality in our lives.

It is, therefore, the part of the brain that supports your state of being which has become innate to you. For me, my state of being for about a decade was that of anxiousness. I had the same thoughts on repeat, creating the same feelings on repeat, creating a habitual anxious state of being. The whole time, I felt powerless to change it because it had become so ingrained in me that I believed it was who I would be forever.

So the process of change requires unlearning old thoughts, relearning new information via your neocortex, new emotions via your limbic brain and through repeating those learnings, you create new habits, embody them, and then they become second nature, thanks to your cerebellum.

We can use our brains to our advantage if we choose to take control over what it is doing. Fun fact. Our brains use more energy than any other part of our body, so to conserve energy, it automates processes, that's why we become creatures of habit. We don't need to think about how we brush our teeth or make a cuppa in the morning, we do it automatically. You need to break the cycles of automation that aren't serving you if you truly wish to transform every area of your life.

20

The Power of the Paradigm

'The subconscious is what a man is, the conscious is what a man knows.'

Neville Goddard

Earlier I shared that there are two levels of the mind: the conscious mind and the subconscious mind. Freud used the metaphor of an iceberg to illustrate these two levels of mind and human personality. He said that the tip of the iceberg represents the conscious mind, but that beneath that in the icy water is the much bigger bulk of the iceberg, representing the subconscious. Freud believed the subconscious to be more important than the conscious and that this exerted the greatest power over our behaviours.

Scientists have seen the brain, but no one has ever seen the invisible mind. As I've already made clear, from our mind comes thoughts and thoughts are the beginning of all creation.

When we are born, we have no conscious mind. The subconscious mind is like a huge open door and everything we see, hear and experience comes pouring in. Think about the sheer number of ideas, thoughts and concepts going into a child's mind during those four to five years of its life. That baby is now a small child programmed to think and behave like the people it's been surrounded by. That small child has made decisions about the world in black and white. This creates their paradigm; a multitude of habits and attitudes programmed into the subconscious mind over and over again. In summary, your paradigm was formed by a repetition of ideas that you heard. We also tend to develop traits that are like our parents too (or whoever raised us) and our human personality begins to form.

The subconscious mind is not a seat of reasoning or creative consciousness, it is strictly a stimulus-response 'play back' device. When an environmental signal is perceived, the subconscious mind automatically activates a previously stored behavioural response – no thinking required! So when we encounter an experience in our life, how we react will be an automatic reflection of what is stored in our subconscious.

Your conscious mind can accept or reject information that comes from the outside and it can also create *new and original ideas*. The conscious mind relies on making sense of the world from observation, experience and education. It finds it difficult to believe what the five senses cannot decode, therefore it only trusts what is coming in via those senses.

Most of us use our mind for *receiving* information, and then accepting or rejecting it, instead of using it for creation. Our Ego puts value on the things that we pay money for. Huge error. As humans living in a consumer-driven world, we put little value on the things that are given to us for free – our powerful mind is given to us at birth for free and consequently we underestimate it.

Conversely, our subconscious mind must accept everything that the conscious mind turns over to it and it can't differentiate between what is *real* and what is *imagined*... Our subconscious mind has no ability to accept or reject information – it will accept anything we give it and is programmed from birth. The subconscious is like the software that we live our lives by.

This subconscious creates our personality which then projects onto the outer world. I've talked about the Law of Attraction and the Law of Vibration. Now I'd like to discuss one of the other laws of the Universe – the Law of Correspondence. This law states that patterns repeat throughout the Universe, and our reality is a projection of what's happening inside us at that moment.

Think of it like this: 'As above, so below. As within, so without'. This beautifully sums up what I've been talking about in this chapter – that whatever we believe inside will reveal itself in our outside world. In order to make a change in our external world, we must first change it internally.

Whatever is impressed on the obedient subconscious mind must be expressed through the body and is responsible for the feelings that are created in our body, predominantly governed by the paradigm we have created. This is why it's often referred to as the emotional mind. When you impress an idea on a subconscious mind, it alters the vibration of the instrument we call our body, a mass of energy that is vibrating at a very high speed.

When we build pictures in our conscious mind, we impress these on our subconscious mind and those are then impressed throughout the body. Remember the thinking/feeling feedback loop we discussed earlier. If we want to impress new information on the subconscious mind, we must think new thoughts, not the same 60,000 thoughts as the day before. We must take time to create and originate new ideas to teach the subconscious. We gotta fake it till we make it, by using our powerful imagination. Then the body moves into action and produces results.

It's incredibly important that you become aware of your current paradigm stored in that subconscious around each area of your life, including friendships, family, money, love and your body. When you can see what you believe about each of these areas, it will give you lifechanging insight into why certain things keep happening in your life.

Back in 2015, I remember reading somewhere online that this guy had made his annual income in one month selling products on Amazon. He excitedly shared on his sales page that it was possible for anyone. My first reaction was that's great – I'm up for it! But I'll be honest, I didn't *really* believe it was possible. I loved the concept but here are a few of the thoughts that really came to the surface that give you an insight into my paradigm.

- 'It won't work for me.'
- 'It must be a scam!'
- 'Very few people in this world can make that sort of money.'
- 'I'm not clever enough.'

This is just a sneak peek into some of my beliefs around money – I can assure you I had a much larger list including things like 'I don't want to have to pay a shit ton of tax' (thanks Mum), 'Rich people are corrupt' (thanks Dad) and that '£50,000 a year is the ultimate salary goal' (thanks society).

As you may be starting to grasp, our paradigms don't even need to be based on fact and they are sweeping generalizations, because as children we see things in black and white and don't have the ability to discern the fact that there are many different contexts. For example, when I hear that rich people are tax-evading bastards, my little brain generalizes those beliefs instead of being able to say, 'Oh, but not *all* are corrupt tax-evading bastards.'

One of the biggest generalized beliefs we create as children is the one that says we aren't good enough. Remember poor old me trying to pass my cycling proficiency test on my purple BMX in the school playground? Well, that was one of those moments that I decided that I simply wasn't good enough. Instead of just thinking that I wasn't able to pass my test on that particular day because clearly the teacher had made a huge mistake, or that perhaps my bike was just a little too big for me at that point, I decided I wasn't good enough. Point blank. These beliefs create mental portraits of how we view ourselves and thus how we go through life.

Then having these negative beliefs impact how we feel in our body, likened to mental indigestion. We experience a situation, the thoughts come in that we aren't good enough, and because as children we can't process it, it gets stuck in our energy body as an emotional blockage. Then when we experience similar situations later in life, it charges that emotional blockage again and we experience it as a feeling of resistance in our body.

Let's say I say to you right now that you can take your annual income and make it your monthly income. Feel into what that brings up for you? Can you feel any constriction or discomfort? This will give you some insight into your own paradigm and your own emotional blocks which can literally be felt in your body.

Your beliefs control your logic. For example, it didn't make sense to me logically how someone could make £20,000 in a month because I had always learned that you get paid by the hour and I'd never seen a job advertised on Indeed.com that offered a full-time, 40-hours-per-week job paying £111 per hour. In fact, I'd never even seen a job that offered more than £150,000 per annum and that was for people who spent half their lives at university.

Talking about the money we earn is weirdly taboo and creates a level of discomfort in people. I started to surround myself with people who were making their annual incomes in one month for the previous four years and began to shift my own discomfort about money, and this resulted in me attracting way more. I hung around with people who would openly share their income and we celebrated them for it. This starts to then impress new beliefs and images onto the subconscious.

I know I've been focusing on money, but it's truly the thing that 99 per cent of people that come to me want to change in some way. Scrap that – not 99 per cent – 100 per cent. Everyone I know would love to have more money, even if they don't want to admit it. Your paradigm is affecting all areas of your life, but the big three are your wealth, your health (and your relationship with food and your body), and lastly your romantic and personal relationships. But before we can change, we need to become aware of it, and this is something that most people will never ever do. Why? Because humanoids spend their whole lives operating unconsciously.

How do we begin to dissect and become aware of the paradigms around the big three areas of our life - health, wealth and relationships? Well, we don't need to go too far – the first place to look is at our parents.

We all come into this world like a sponge, and we suck up all of the information that we can as we grow up. If you are born into a loveless marriage like me, or brought up with parents who worked every minute to survive, like me, or were allowed to eat two chicken sandwich meals at McDonald's, like me again – then what do you think our little sponge brains are going to be sucking up about life?

When you put a sponge in a bowl of dirty dishwater and then squeeze that sponge, what comes out? Well, dirty dishwater. Most of us carry around dirty dishwater – or negative paradigms of those who brought us into their world. It's not their fault – they didn't realize they were doing it because it's a cycle of generational conditioning and most people never read the stuff I'm teaching you in this book, so never become aware.

One thing I love to do with my clients is to get them to really think about what they saw, heard and experienced as a child around those areas of their life. I'll share some of mine to get you thinking about this.

Food

My parents are Middle Eastern and food and family is a big thing. We would congregate around huge family feasts which my mum would spend all day preparing. My mum's family are feeders. I'll never forget spending summers with my grandmother and aunties, who lived in Sweden, and every five minutes they would ask if we wanted something else to eat. They literally couldn't bear the thought that anyone would ever be hungry for a single moment. My mum would often tell us to finish our plates because it was a 'waste of food', so I got used to eating everything on my plate even if I was completely full. My mum also never ever said 'enough'. Portion control was not a concept in my darling mother's brain. When she would sneak us to McDonald's (it wasn't halal so we couldn't tell Dad!) she would let us enjoy the McChicken sandwich. Although, I never ever seemed to feel satisfied after just one meal deal, so she would let me have another. Do you know how many calories are in that?! The point being as a child I was never really taught portion control. By the time I was 16 I was at war with my body and weight, and this caused so many issues buying clothes. This started a decade long battle with my body which included cabbage soup diets, dodgy diet pills bought off eBay and I even considered eating cotton wool thanks to an article I read in a magazine about what models did to stay slim. It never once occurred to me back then, that my beliefs around food were keeping me in a negative cycle, nor was I given the knowledge that if I could change those beliefs, I could control my weight. That's why what I am teaching is so important to you.

What did you hear, see and experience around food as a child?

Money

Let's talk about money now. As you know I didn't grow up in a wealthy household and there are moments that are etched in my mind which taught me about money. One of those was being ten years old and so desperately wanting this top from Gap that had a star in the middle. All the cool kids had them and would all wear matching on own clothes day at school. I begged my mum and she said it was too expensive. The crippling thing about being in a private school was that most of the parents there were wealthy. They had enormous houses with big drives and took ski holidays to Meribel, half-term trips on Sunsail vacations and spent the summer in Vale de Lobo in Portugal. These were the kind of holiday places reserved for posh people. We couldn't afford this, so we would look on Teletext for a last-minute bargain to wherever the budget could stretch.

My mum was always looking for a sale and, even to this day, she will admit she has some sort of shopping disease when she sees an offer, she cannot help but purchase it. If you go into her larder, you find at last two of everything. Growing up with a religious dad, we were accustomed to giving to charity. There was always a jar in our house that he filled, and I would always hear, 'But there's poor people everywhere', and this constant guilt that we should never want for more. My dad also had an open dislike for wealthy people. He was a lawyer and he came across a lot of shady wealthy people, and he saw them all as 'corrupt, tax evading bastards'. My dad never earned that much as a lawyer because he chose to help people that couldn't afford legal help, and this was subsidised by the government. He was openly honest about how he couldn't ever charge £200 an hour like other lawyers. To my mum money should never be wasted and to my dad, money should only be spent on very few high-quality things and the rest to go to charity.

What did you hear, see and experience around money as a child?

Relationships

I've already disclosed to you that I was born into a loveless marriage. I don't really have any memories of my parents showing affection to one another, and I can't tell you the amount of time I would sit on the stairs in my first house overhearing my parents arguing. I can't even remember what they argued about – but I knew they weren't right together. When I was ten, they decided to have another baby – because perhaps this would be the glue that could stick two people who were completely wrong for each other together. I can tell you now, a baby isn't glue. A baby causes sleep deprivation, cries and shits. They finally divorced when my baby brother was two.

Our parents' relationship is our first and most influential example of how to interact and communicate in a romantic relationship. Studies have also shown the ways in which anger and conflict are managed in your family of origin also play a large part in how we communicate with adult romantic partners.

What did you hear, see and experience around relationships as a child?

Tony Robbins puts forward the theory that we subconsciously seek to identify with the primary caregiver whose love we craved most, even if they have passed away, we shape ourselves into what we think we need to be in order to gain their love, their acceptance and their approval. This craving for love heavily influences our identity, even as an adult, and understanding this can help you better understand your personality. You have created your identity from your childhood and from those who raised you, so those are the beliefs you will always align yourself with.

Think of the person whose love you craved most as a child: who did you need to be for that person to accept and love you? What did you have to think or do to gain their approval? Sometimes the answer is simple, sometimes it's more complex.

By examining your childhood and understanding whose love you craved most, you can get a clearer explanation of why you see yourself the way you do. You can also examine your relationships and access a better understanding of how they've succeeded or failed in the past.

Are you constantly trying to prove to your partner that you're worthy, because your parents made you feel that you needed to do so for their love?

Craving affection is not a bad thing, but by understanding why you make the emotional decisions you do, based on your upbringing, you can acknowledge what it is that makes you tick and work to change the behaviours you're unhappy with.

So what does this have to do with you living your purpose?

Well, how can you live your best, most fulfilled life if you are plagued with all the limited programming that you inherited from your childhood? How can you make the movie of your life become a cinematic masterpiece, if the projector is faulty and only shows half a picture in black and white? What most adults don't realize is they are walking around in seemingly older physical bodies but still acting and behaving as a result of the beliefs that their inner child created. That is why, without realizing it, we repeat the same dysfunctional relationships, with money and our bodies, instead of taking the action to change them.

Willpower is not enough to make big changes because there's so much going on in your unconscious mind that you are – well – not conscious of. Most psychologists would agree that any personal change starts with self-awareness – something that sadly most people lack. But my aspiration for you as you go through this book and start living a life *on purpose*, not on autopilot, is that you start to identify where patterns of thoughts, feelings and communications originate.

Take a moment to pause reading and reflect on your childhood. Try to remember the patterns you had in interacting with your parents. If you can start to become conscious of these patterns then you can start truly living life where you aren't mindlessly plodding through, allowing decades to pass wondering if anything will ever change.

Every one of us is the sum total of our own thoughts. We are where we are because that's exactly where we feel we deserve to be based on our programming. Every single one of us must live off the result of our subconscious thoughts, because what you think today, tomorrow, next week or next month moulds your life. The change therefore starts from within you. I can tell you from having worked with so many incredible humans that once you start this process there's no going back. And the possibilities are endless. Now isn't that exciting?

21

Beware of the Boogeyman

Human beings are a unique species because we can turn on our stress responses *just by thought alone*. Yes, when children think about the fictional boogeyman, the thought alone can result in a very real and palpable physical experience that is no different than if a real life boogeyman was stood right in front of them. Unfortunately, this isn't limited to children, adults can also turn on a stress response from thought alone too and this includes remembering traumatic events of the past or worrying about future events that haven't even occurred.

Thoughts send chemical signals like little messengers that then make your body feel exactly the way it would if the situation was happening in real time, even if the thought is from 20 years ago or *hasn't even happened at all...* This is one of the most powerful things you need to grasp – that we can literally create fear and anxiety out of thin air with a momentary thought. If you have fearful thoughts, then you will start to feel fear. From the second you feel the fear, that then causes a feedback loop to your brain via your emotions.

We can have bad memories triggered by seeing someone or something of the past, we can have fears of the future ignited by an unexpected experience, and our bodies can have a full on physical response. Every time I thought about my closest friends being sexually abused and the moment that they told me, I *felt* deep sadness (thank you chemical messengers). It wasn't happening in real time, but it sure as fuck felt the same. This physical reaction in the body (the feeling) then generates more thoughts equal to how you were feeling. This caused me to spiral into a negative compilation of thoughts, releasing more chemicals, making me feel MORE of the way I've been thinking. This is a feedback loop that happens on automation which reinforces your state of being. Your body literally becomes a reflection of your mind.

This cycle of feeling, thinking, feeling, thinking conditions the body to that state. When you think and behave in the same way (for example, thinking anxious thoughts and then behaving in a way that an anxious person may behave), you begin to programme yourself. This then becomes your identity, which determines your personality (which is what you think, act and feel) which then creates your personal reality and the end product is that you stay the same person. Can you start to see how thoughts have a profound effect on how we change our lives and how most of ours stay in a negative state so automatically?

I had conditioned my body into a state of depression and anxiety, which coincidentally actually led to me having some other physical ailments related to my gut for many years – science has shown that the gut is powerfully connected to your emotions and the brain.

We also really love to prove ourselves right. If we believe we are a depressed person, for example, every time we think depressing thoughts we will then confirm that identity. We then also look for examples in our outer world to confirm this identity.

So the first step is to become conscious of those unconscious hardwired thoughts, because **we can change them**. The science of neuroplasticity and epigenetics has proven this. We need to become aware of the thoughts and emotions that have become feedback mechanisms. But in order to change we need to be greater than our environment and our bodies.

We need to see past those automated thoughts.

We need to use our thoughts to *create* rather than to react and respond.

We cannot change our personal reality with the same personality. **We have to become someone else.**

The fact we are able to witness our thoughts, consciously be aware of them and see them as an observer is a sign that those thoughts are not all ours. In fact, witnessing those thoughts as a curious observer is the first step in bringing down the Shitty Committee board meetings. Challenging negative thought patterns takes discipline and mastery, but as you gain this, the Shitty Committee loses its strength. When we take ownership of our thoughts and choose to replace damaging thoughts with empowering thoughts, we begin to rip apart the very threads that have held our paradigm together.

When you can observe a thought without putting energy behind it, you are no longer the hardwired program, you are the consciousness observer. When you have the ability to witness a thought and recognize it is just part of a feedback loop that has been manufactured in your body, you are demonstrating metacognition. **Metacognition is, put simply, thinking about one's thinking.**

When you become observant of who you no longer want to be, you start to break the programming that is connected to your 'old self'. You make the brain work differently, and this is when we can start to see change.

The reason so many people are humanoids is because day in, day out, they are simply not making new choices or creating new thoughts. As I've reiterated multiple times, new thoughts lead to new emotions, that lead to new behaviours and new experiences. We become a new person. Since our environments provide the external stimuli that are decoded (by your five senses) which result in the same thoughts, which then starts the same feedback loop of emotions in your body – we cannot rely on what is happening in our 3D world to help us change. We need to go beyond what we see with our five senses – we need to start thinking fourth dimensionally and use our incredible imaginations.

22

The Quantum Playing Field

'Close your eyes and focus on your breath.' I listened as Dr Joe Dispenza instructed us in the auditorium packed with fans who had flocked to see him live in action in London. I felt every muscle relax in my body and I remained focused on the darkness.

'Become nobody, in no space, with no time.'

Welcome to the quantum playing field: where infinite possibilities are available, where creation begins.

Where nothing turns into something.

Where thought energy turns into 3D reality.

When we close our eyes and walk boldly into the quantum field, we are in a space of creation.

> 'A thought is a substance, producing the thing that is imagined by the thought.'
>
> *Wallace D. Wattles*

During our everyday lives, it would be logical to say that our waking consciousness is governed by our five senses. When we enter a different state of consciousness or start thinking fourth dimensionally, it's the place we go where our senses are shut down and aren't decoding information of the external world. When we enter the quantum field we are no longer defined by the space around us and the linear time we experience when our eyes are open. This is the creative playing field where all things are created from.

To our logical mind and our senses, reality is confined to the instant that we call *Now*. To our brain, this very moment seems to contain the whole of reality, everything else isn't real; the past and the future are purely imaginary. My past is just a snapshot image of memory of things that have happened and the future simply does not exist yet, even though when I close my eyes, I can visualize it in Technicolor.

Before everything was created in the physical world, it was first imagined in someone's mind, therefore it can be suggested that everything in the Universe occurs twice: once in the mind of humans and then in physical reality.

'To what we will call the fourth-dimensional focus, the past, the present, and the future of the natural mind are a present whole.'

Neville Goddard

This quote refers to thinking beyond the 3D world we perceive. When we can focus fourth dimensionally, we can access the past, the present and the future all as one. The third dimension is always bounded by a linear understanding of time; the third dimension is always present and holds no future or past. The fourth dimension goes beyond our senses and our natural mind of reasoning and logic and the new 'depth' presented in the fourth dimension is time. We can time travel when we close our eyes!

You can be, have and do whatever you want here – there are no limits and no time or space limitations. You can be on a white sandy beach in beautiful Bora Bora sipping mai tais, or freezing your booty off in Skegness with a bright blue bottle of WKD. You can be transported ten years into the future or gallivanting in the memories of 20 years into the past. Whatever floats your boat, honey. In this place, you can be free to use your imagination controlled by desire.

We have been given the ability to close our eyes, to imagine, to visualize. We have the neurocircuitry to be able to do that for a reason: **so that we can create our reality and manifest our desires**.

What is manifesting? Simply put, 'to manifest' means 'to see in physical form that which you have thought of'. You use your mental faculties to create a picture in your mind of your desires and then use your physical body to make it come to fruition. This isn't magic and does involves physical action.

However, it's like we have been given a wand that we never use, because we never got taught how to switch it on. Surely closing my eyes and imagining my dream life into fruition is way too simple? *No one can change their lives from such a simple act?!*

Well, I'm sorry dear humanoids, we are programmed to believe that life is hard, that we must work every hour to create success so the cognitive dissonance that it could be this simple is real. Having spent the best part of a decade studying this stuff, the sheer amount of stories from people who have changed their lives by using their thoughts has literally quashed any scepticism I have ever had.

The phenomenon of thought deserves a moment of recognition. It's not fully understood and seen as a mental action, but everything around us is a thought or idea that has come to materialization through the creative work of a human being. We cannot do anything in life without a preceding thought impulse. It is the generating force behind everything!

No amount of physical manipulation in the physical world will create the life we want. All the work is done on the inside, in our minds. Imagine picking a gorgeous Pink Lady apple off a tree and thinking, 'Damn, I wish this was an orange'. It doesn't matter what you try to do in the physical world, including trying to paint it orange, you will never be able change the truth that this is, in fact, an apple. The only way you get to pick a juicy Spanish orange is by planting a seed and by giving that seed the right soil, sun and water to grow. That seed is your thought.

Let me caveat this by saying that this is the first step, and by no means the final one, to changing your life. Spending time envisioning what we truly want from our life is the first of five steps of the life-changing Manifesting Method. But we are so used to believing only that which we see, or that which our senses can perceive, that we become blind to the possibilities. I cannot wait to show you what lies beyond your own mind and the capabilities you have, because I know with every ounce of my Soul that this can help you too.

In order to be able to run freely in the quantum field of all possibilities with no time and no space, we need to make the deliberate decision to separate our mind from our senses and use our mind creatively, consciously and intentionally – putting our attention fully on 'just being' with our spirit. This is the definition to me of being spiritual:

> The ability to disconnect from what our physical senses can perceive and connect with our non-physical part – our pure potential – so that we can create a life better than our fucking dreams.

23
Daydreaming

'If Noor would just focus more instead of daydreaming, she would
do so much better at school.'

I would hear that a lot from my disapproving teachers at parents'
evenings.

By the time I was a teenager, I'd turned daydreaming into a
fine art, especially when it came to boys. Despite the fact I didn't
think I was particularly attractive, I somehow managed to manifest
being with almost every boy I had a crush on. I can tell you now
that if you invest enough energy and time into visualizing every
detail of every hypothetical date, and even your wedding day and
kids, that vision is likely going to manifest. Of course, we cannot
control other people's free will, but if you feel a potential connection there – it is most likely possible! Trying to manifest that a
celebrity you have never met will fall in love with you, will be met
with great difficulty because they don't even know you exist, but
if you have met someone and felt a spark, that could happen. But
this comes with a word of warning: the reality of being with the
partner is often vastly different from the daydream!

For the daydreaming/creative visualization to work, it's imper-
ative to see a scene in your mind that means that your desire has
been fulfilled. For example, if you wanted to move to your dream
home, you wouldn't imagine the sale, you would imagine having
Christmas in that house, surrounded by family in your new living
room, filling your bellies with a full festive dinner. Bring in all the
sensations as though you are actually in that moment. Bring in
what you can hear, see, smell and feel.

I have so many stories of how things have come to manifest in my life and I share those throughout this book, but there's one that truly gives me goosebumps every time I tell it, because it shows with total certainty that this shit works.

It was June 2017, and I was walking the streets of New York to meet one of my best friends for brunch at a French place in Manhattan. The sun was shining and I was recounting how incredible my first live event in the USA had gone and how much I wanted to do more. As I embarked on the 30-minute walk to meet my friend I decided to listen to Jen Sincero's *You Are a Badass*. I remember how it felt to listen to her speak and, in the confines of my own heart and soul, my desire to be an author was cemented. I would daydream about signing a book deal and sharing the news with my friends and family.

As I listened to her book, soaking in every word that came into my ears, I imagined what it would be like to be an author like Jen and daydreamed about the book deal that was so close to my heart and I wanted to manifest. I had never told a soul about this secret desire to become an author like Jen. It was way too cringey to say out loud, because the dream felt like it was something that would take years to accomplish. However, I spent the next seven months dedicated to seeing how I could take steps to making this dream a reality. Little did I know that the Universe was working its magic and one of my amazing clients had worked in publishing for two decades. She really believed in me, more than anyone ever had, and she said she would love to help me. Each day I would spend time daydreaming about how it would feel to be a signed book author. Even after every rejection that knocked me slightly, I held the faith and expected that my time would come. I knew in my heart that this desire was meant for me and that, through following my intuition and taking action, the Universe could deliver.

Desire is a powerful thing and when it's true in your heart, it will propel you forward. Desire is simply an awareness of something we lack or need to make our lives more fulfilled and enjoyable. For me writing was a vehicle for me to serve others, and this has always been porn for my soul. When we daydream about getting what we want in the fourth dimensional space, where we can create whatever the fuck we want, our spiritual self finds a way to make it happen.

Fast forward to 2 March 2018. I received a forwarded thread of emails from my client Jessica, from my lovely editor Jonathan. I literally couldn't even believe what I was reading, a sign from the Universe so strong that it brought me to tears. And it confirmed everything that I ever believed about desire.

> 'I'd love to bring Noor and *You've Got This* to the same list as Jen Sincero's *You Are A Badass*.'

(*You've Got This* was the PG-rated working title of my first book *Just F*cking Do It!*)

I was offered a book deal by the same publishers that represented Jen Sincero in the UK and the email continued to say they had been looking for a British version of Jen and they believed it could be me. From that moment on, I knew that the Universe really was listening and my faith catapulted to dizzy new heights.

This whole experience helped me trust even deeper in all the concepts I've been teaching you in this book. Learning to have faith in unseen and intangible forces is something I had found incredibly difficult my whole life, but slowly and surely the series of synchronicities and signs in my life confirming that there was 'something' out there listening to me, were indeed starting to mount up.

24
Expect and Attract

Cultivating the incredible habit of daydreaming, as we did as children, and fuelling that vision with as much sensory energy so that it feels real, sets in motion something pretty freaking special and we can take our desires that we think about and begin to witness them coming to fruition in real life. However, how we manifest is governed by a set of Universal Laws.

The first is the Law of Expectancy. When you go out for a nice meal and place your order with the waitress, you don't sit there wishing and hoping and praying that the waitress will bring your meal to your table. You drink your wine, catch up with whoever is joining you and have full faith and expectation that your meal will arrive. Expectancy is a crucial ingredient as it demonstrates faith. Most people visualize their desires and then think of all the reasons why it won't come. They spend each day thinking 'Where is the *insert desire*?' instead of expecting it, like that meal you ordered. Every time you do this, you put a metaphorical middle finger up to the Universe and block the flow of energy and slow down the progress.

When we have faith, we align energetically with the vibration of the desired outcome. 'The experience of the end wills the man,' states Neville Goddard. It takes practice and discipline to be able to visualize and create a state of being that is aligned with the future outcome rather than stay stuck in thoughts of an unwanted past, or being scared that the desire won't come and it will all fall apart in a fearful future.

When we decide on what we truly want, and imagine it in our mind, those thoughts then emit energy-in-motion (emotions) at different frequencies.

This is a good moment to delve deeper into one of the more popular spiritual laws of the Universe that you may or may not have heard of. If this Universal Law was a person, then it hired the best publicist and has managed to impact the lives of many people. It's the law in the cool club: the Law of Attraction. Unfortunately, due to its mass popularization, the Law of Attraction has been misunderstood and, like a game of Chinese whispers, it has been interpreted as a magical process where all you need to do is think of what you want and BAM, there it is. **LOUD buzzer signalling NO goes off**

I hate to be the bearer of bad news, but I was one of the players in that game of Chinese whispers and the danger with this misconception is that this powerful and life-changing law of the Universe is more complex than it's purported to be. Therefore it is misunderstood and, consequently, poo-pooed by people who don't understand how to make it work or who don't get immediate magical results.

It's also one of many laws of the Universe that are widely known and works in conjunction with its counterparts. I shared earlier in the book about the Law of Vibration – that everything in this Universe is vibratory and nothing rests. The second concept to grasp is that vibrations of similar frequency are drawn together. A great way to see this is to think about two drops of water that are slowly moving toward each other. When they get close enough, they pull together like little magnets and – boom – two become one (cue Spice Girls in the background).

Now, think of putting water and oil close together, no matter how close you put a drop of oil to a drop of water, they will not combine because they are too different on a vibrational level. Think about humans, we connect with people we are similar to, that we 'vibe with' – similar vibrations are attracted to one another.

This is the foundation which the Law of Attraction is based on. If you want to bring about something in your life, regardless of what that thing is, you need to begin vibrating at a level that is congruent with your desired reality. When we enter a meditative

state and are able to focus on the fact we are pure consciousness, we can take our attention off time and space, forget about
our physical body and we can walk toward the quantum playing
field where all of creation starts. The little electrical signals we call
thoughts impress themselves on the creative field of the Universe.
They are neurotransmitters deciding what you will create in your
physical reality.

But it doesn't stop there. Our thoughts continually need to be in
vibrational alignment with our desired reality. Our thoughts create the vibration in our body, so this is why trying to fake thinking
positive thoughts when we are feeling negative will never give the
desired result. But when we do it right, it is what I call tuning into
Universe FM. Once we gain the ability to condition our minds to
our desired frequencies of vibration, our physical reality quickly
follows suit and reflects back to us our new vibration.

In *The Strangest Secret* by Earl Nightingale, we are presented
with a parable in which he describes the human mind as being
much like a farmer's land. He says the land gives the farmer a
choice. They may plant in that land whatever they choose. 'The
land doesn't care what is planted. It's up to the farmer to make the
decision. The mind, like the land, will return what you plant, but
it doesn't care what you plant.' He goes on to say that if a farmer
plants two seeds, one a seed of corn, the other nightshade (a deadly
poison), waters and takes care of the land, what will happen? The
land will grow the deadly poison in just as wonderful abundance
as it will the corn. This is exactly the same as the mind, and the
human mind is far more fertile, more incredible and mysterious
than the land, and it works the same way.

Earl Nightingale explains that our minds truly don't care what
we plant. It could be phenomenal success or it could be constant
failure. It may be a life-changing worthwhile goal, or fear, anxiety
and confusion. Whatever we plant will 100 per cent grow.

Earlier I explained how the conscious mind has the ability to
accept, reject and originate new thoughts. When we don't become
aware of how to use our conscious mind, we are just reacting and

responding to the outside world and our subconscious beliefs are unconsciously dictating the vibration of our body and, consequently, what we attract (or repel) into our life.

You may consciously think you want more money, but if your paradigm is fearful of money, that fear will be creating a fear vibration in your body that is not in alignment with your desire for money.

So how do you begin to make sure your subconscious beliefs and identity align with your future desire? Thinking alone is not enough for energetic shifts and change to happen. We need to get emotionally involved in the idea, which simply means you need to truly feel into the thought. Imagining your goal and allowing yourself to truly feel how it would be if the thought was already a physical manifestation is the key to start creating changes.

You can consciously try to think positively, but it doesn't produce positive results unless you can feel it. Our mind learns through repetition, so when we intentionally use our conscious mind to create new thoughts about the future, and use repetition to start reprogramming our mind, over time a new identity is formed.

We become what we think about.

When we have faith, we feel empowered to decide what we want in our life and go for it without fear. This is easier said than done, because our good friend fear has been sat in the passenger seat of our life for so long, assuring us that things will go wrong if we dare to venture to new and beautiful unknown pastures. But without faith, we cannot find peace. Without faith, we cannot learn to surrender to the beautiful process of growth. Without faith, we will always live life just dipping our toes into our dreams, without ever really diving deep into the desires that are meant for us.

25
I'm Leaving You

It was 4 am and I woke up because I thought my heart was about to explode out of my chest. Richard was not there. I had spoken with him at 1am and he had said he was on his way home. He had only been 10 minutes away, so where the hell was he? My heart was racing, my head was spinning, and I must have called him 1000 times.

'Is he dead?!' or, even worse than death, 'Is he cheating on me?!'

I locked the front door so he couldn't get in and I waited, every second trying to breathe through my anxiety. I was enraged, barely able to catch my breath. Our baby was innocently deep asleep upstairs.

I finally let him in 20 minutes later and grabbed his phone.

'If you can't use it to text me,' I screamed, 'then you shouldn't have one, because clearly you can't operate it!'

I threw the phone on the floor in rage, but unfortunately it bounced off the carpet and hit the plant pot and smashed. Oops.

'I am leaving you – I cannot do this anymore!'

I loved him more than anything and knew he was who I was meant to be with, but it felt I was on a battlefield with him and my anxiety and I didn't have the weapons to win. He had decided to stay out longer as lads do; he didn't see the harm because I was just going back to sleep and he couldn't fathom why I was so angry that it resulted in a smashed phone.

I can tell you now, it got a lot worse with Richard before it got better and the words 'I'm leaving you' came out of my mouth many times in the first five years we were together. It felt like he didn't want to grow up, even though he was a dad now. He chose to spend time with people who constantly cheated on their partners and felt like it was okay. I had difficulty being accepted by his family. Here was the man I loved, the father of my child and all I kept thinking was 'I'm going to be a single mother', because I didn't like the person I was when we were together. I didn't want to be an anxious wreck for my daughter. I spent hours crying, thinking 'Why is it so hard? Why is nothing ever easy for me?'.

This had been a continuous pattern in every relationship that I couldn't seem to win. When I look back to those times and what we are like now, it is like looking at two very different people. Two people who loved each other very much and knew they were meant to be together. But one wasn't ready to grow up and the other was battling with their own anxiety and depression.

Even though I was finally a mother, I felt like I was failing my daughter because I didn't have my shit together. I thought when I met the love of my life, it would be like glitter and rainbows and roses every day. I'd wanted a fairytale that did not exist for me.

My Soul had lessons to learn, pain to overcome and growth to experience. Richard was one of my greatest teachers and sometimes those lessons were harder pills to swallow than the Prozac. But, oh my gosh, the beautiful relationship we have created now, the three beautiful kids and the growth we have both had to experience has been an incredible journey. When I look back at everything we went through, the lessons were so clear.

My 'happy ever after' didn't happen like a fairytale. My 'happy ever after' came with a shit load of tears, late-night arguments and a smashed iPhone. It also came with honesty, growth and the birth of three children over 11 years.

I don't want my children to miss out on life because they think it needs to all be perfect and they should only strive for happy moments.

I don't want them to fear the growth that two humans may need to go through to find a 'happy ever after'. Living *on purpose* means deciding who you want in your life and what you are willing to do to make those relationships work.

We need to experience the full breadth and spectrum of the human experience with courage, rather than hiding to avoid the pain.

I want them to understand that sometimes the most beautiful things can start off messy and confusing, but if two people are willing to take 100 per cent responsibility to make their lives count, and their relationship work, then huge shifts can start to happen. It all starts with using your imagination to focus on how you want your future to be, not what you do not want it to be. It involves becoming present with now instead of worrying about the past or the future.

26

Faith Over Fear

My eyes were filled with tears and I could feel my chest tighten, but I didn't want to let Maria know I was crying. The fact I'd consumed what felt like seven pints of vodka and soda wasn't helping, but I happen to cry at Pampers adverts, so listening to yet another amazing woman share her sadness that they are in an ongoing battle with making their dream of being a mother a reality, tipped me over the edge.

I listened to the sadness of her miscarrying and the unimaginable pain of having to terminate a second pregnancy because of serious issues that were found on scans.

'I literally had to push it out' she said as I tried to process what she was telling me.

I had heard of mothers doing this, but had never sat in front of someone who I knew and truly thought was a special person and listened first-hand about such a traumatizing experience.

'I'm okay. If I am not meant to be a mother, then that's the way it is. I'm fine about it,' she said with such positivity that it made me want to cry more because we are always told to put on a brave face in life.

But I have coached enough people to see past brave faces. I could see the doubt and fear crippling her faith.

Of course, it had. She is only human and has experienced the loss of now two pregnancies.

I know what doubt does to someone. I know when someone underplays their true desires because they are so scared of admitting how much they want something. I know because I've done it many times.

'Would you be open to me sharing an observation?' I asked whilst holding back my tears.

'Yes of course.'

I looked at her tentatively, worried about what the potential outcome of what I was about to say could be.

'I know you are saying you don't mind if you become a mother or not and that you have made peace...but is that true?' I paused.

'My gut is telling me that your fear is guiding your decision. I think you would be the most amazing mother and despite everything you have been through I don't want you to lose faith.'

Tears started streaming down her face.

Shit, I'd made her cry.

She had hidden her pain behind a gorgeous bright smile and sunny disposition for so long. She had used positivity as a weapon against her vulnerability.

I hugged her and I couldn't hold back the tears as I held this beautiful human while she courageously let go of the brave face. I wondered whether opening Pandora's Box after a bottle of gin was the best time or should this conversation have happened whilst sober. Or maybe it was the perfect time. The gin broke down a barrier.

We mustn't be scared to feel as humans.

We mustn't be scared to say our biggest dreams even if we have been so hurt in the past.

'I am sorry for crying and being silly!' she said.

'Never ever ever fucking apologize for feeling. You deserve the world and I just want you to know that there's no room for doubt in this. You need to fully believe that it's possible, and not allow the past to dictate what will happen in the future. You can make this happen.'

We hugged and cried and hugged some more.

As humans we should never apologize for feeling. We should never apologize for wanting what we want. We should hold space for vulnerability. Living *on purpose* means being non-negotiable about our dreams and relentlessly figuring out what could be going on at a deeper level that may be stopping us. Maria had no physical reason that she couldn't conceive naturally. And I urged her to work with someone on the emotional blockages that could be stopping her.

'It's okay to say, "I want this, but I am scared",' I said through the snot whilst wiping my tears away. 'It's okay if things don't pan out like a fairytale.'

When they left I sat on my kitchen side and cried to Richard. I hadn't drunk gin in a decade because it made me emotional and my mother-in-law told me it was often referred to as mother's ruin! And here I was, sat on my kitchen side, sobbing, feeling ruined.

I cried for all the women who are struggling to become mothers.

I cried because I know I am blessed and I never take it for granted. I cried with gratitude.

I also cried because so many women will never be taught how their emotions and trauma in the body could be stopping them and that there are so many incredible solutions that they will never know about.

And then I stopped crying and smiled, because I did know the answers and I knew that, even in this book, I would be able to share so much insight with people so that they too can understand this link. I went to bed with a full heart and woke up with a sore head, but I remembered that seeing her pain made me more determined to help others.

Pain can be turned into power.

Pain can be turned into something positive, as long as we can be honest.

Life is messy and beautiful and sometimes we just need to be around people who let us say our dreams in spite of our fears, and are there to hug us when we cry and let us know it will all be okay.

27
Masks

It started with a kiss.

My shoes were sticking to the floor that was decorated with cheap vodka and Red Bull, courtesy of the freshers living their best lives at the student union. He was wearing a shirt that had 'Muff Diver' printed on its back – which should have been the warning sign from day one.

One kiss turned into a fling of drunken nights, cinema trips and adult sleepovers. He was the kinda boy that when you were with him, you never wanted the day or night to end, but when you were without him, you were left a bag of nerves questioning every moment, dissecting every conversation, rereading every text message wondering what you did so wrong to have resulted in not hearing from him in days. G made me become a very strange person, weak at the knees and a sucker to impress him wherever I could.

One day he excitedly told me he had tickets to go see Faithless in concert. I had zero like in Faithless, but before I had a chance to even contemplate what was about to come out of my mouth, almost like an involuntary spasm of the tongue, I excitedly replied, 'OMG, I have tickets to go too – we should all go together!'

What the actual fuck is wrong with you Noor – why did you say that?!

The worst thing wasn't that I was now a pathological liar, but that now I would have to pay £50 out of my dwindling student loan to purchase a ticket to a concert that I wouldn't even enjoy. I also had to force one of my housemates to come – to which she agreed if I paid for her ticket too. But it was okay, I told myself. G would like me even more because now we loved the same music and could go to concerts together forever. And the night would end being so utterly magical that the £100 dent in my depleting bank account would be worth it. First red flag – when you think you need to constantly impress someone, this means that on some level you do not think you are worthy of them just as you are.

As fate had it, G got a stomach bug on that night, was understandably anti-social, and then left after the first hour. I was left enduring listening to a band I didn't even like. 'That'll teach you for being a moron,' I cursed myself. To add insult to Faithless injury, as abruptly as he arrived in my life, Muff Diver disappeared off the face of the earth without a word.

Eight months after he went AWOL, I saw his name appear on my MSN messenger (where did that ever go?) and as I sat in the internet café on the strip in Malia, heart pounding at the mere sight that he was online, he typed, 'Hello stranger'.

HELLO?! Where the fuck did you disappear to all those months ago?! Did you not know I spent £100 on a fucking concert that I didn't even enjoy for you!?

But instead of putting my own self-worth first, I was sucked back into his flirtatious Welsh charm and witty banter, and I remembered how gorgeous, funny and kind he was. I'm sure he went AWOL for a completely plausible reason. This messenger chat revealed he had moved into the house almost exactly behind mine. It was meant to be – *it had to be fate that brought us back together.*

One autumn evening, one online convo resulted in me knocking on his door in my pyjamas at 9pm, armed with a pack of digestive biscuits and a bottle of red wine. That night turned into months and I fell in love with him. However, I knew from the get-go that this boy was not looking for a relationship. For months I convinced myself that I was totally okay with this and portrayed that persona every time I saw G. Red flag number two – lying to yourself usually doesn't work out well.

Most people are familiar with presenting a certain face to the world, and at that moment I was wearing a mask. We all do it to some extent and that does not mean we are being fake; it just means we don't feel comfortable fully being ourselves. In fact, during the course of any given day, we can use a variety of different masks as a social disguise to help get us through different situations in life. Mine was the mask of the cool girl who was completely happy with being a friend with benefits. It was fucking exhausting.

Masks are heavy and they confuse us as we don't know who we are when we are wearing them. Trying to live our most authentic and aligned life requires us to be brutally honest and trust those intuitive hits of wisdom. My wisdom was saying, 'Noor, walk away', but my fearful Ego, that craved validation and lived in stress of being single forever, kept stringing me along for the ride. Plus, I was in madly in love.

How many of us live life behind a mask or a myriad of masks depending on the context? A mask of self-assuredness, confidence, authority, perfection, efficiency, etc., while hiding who we truly are or what's really going on for us?

The biggest problem is that when we get accustomed to wearing a mask, we lose ourselves in the process of trying to please others. The manager that feels the need to be authoritative in the workplace, but is a riot on a Friday with friends to blow off all the steam of being stern all week. The mum who acts like she's perfect in front of the school gates but drinks a bottle of merlot each night to keep her sanity. The girlfriend who puts the needs of her boyfriend first and cries herself to sleep every night because she's deeply unhappy. The husband who is having an affair but looks his wife in the eyes and says she's the only one. The person who nods and says yes to everything, when they really want to say no.

I know I wore a mask around my dad for years. I felt this invisible need to please him and make sure he was proud of me. How many of us bow down to societal expectations? Whose life are you actually living? Denying your authentic self from coming through drains your energy. Where in life are you not speaking your truth for fear of repercussions?

Too many of us go through life thinking that we are not good enough, smart enough, funny enough as we are, so we put on an invisible mask. This lack of enough is a virus. Scared that if others saw the 'real you' behind the mask, they would judge. I held back from ever truly expressing how G made me feel when he wouldn't message for days. I simply couldn't find the courage to walk away and accept that this was not going to work out long term. I would berate myself for not having the courage to be honest, for being so weak. I never told him about my anxiety, because G was too cool to have an anxious girlfriend, so the love I had for him was always masked with this underlying sense of distress for me. He was honestly a truly great guy, but I was holding on to a fantasy and I felt ashamed that behind closed doors I was a hot mess.

'Shame is the intensely painful feeling or experience of believing we are flawed and therefore unworthy of acceptance and belonging,' says Brené Brown, and as I grew older I realized this was the theme that had been haunting me ever since I was a child. Rarely, does a person emerge from childhood unscathed from the conditioning of their parents. I couldn't shake this sinking feeling that I wasn't important enough in G's life and this resulted in my anxiety escalating. *Why was I broken? Why couldn't I be like other normal girls who didn't feel like this in a relationship?*

I felt I had to wear a mask around G, to be the girlfriend I imagined *he wanted me to be.* I was living up to a false expectation that I had created in my own mind. The type of girl that didn't care if her boyfriend didn't message for days, the type of girl that never moaned about him being out till 3am, the girl who was okay with being seventh on the list of things in his life.

My whole life was so fixated on whether the future would work out, that I honestly forgot to live in the moment. I would convince myself each week, I would need to break up with him to save the pain I was causing myself, but every moment he walked back through that door with his leather jacket and beaming smile, I would fall in love all over again and hoped that one day I would stop feeling like this.

This was a lie I would tell myself so often that I decided to quit working for Club 18–30 (again) and tried to get a proper job in the UK. I got my own place in Cardiff so I could live near G. I would wear the mask of a girl who had her shit together, but the minute I got drunk, the mask would fall off and I couldn't hold back the tears, and I'd cause arguments. These fiery moments would meet my need for love and connection on street corners while up to my neck in vodka and coke.

We all have six needs we will simultaneously meet consistently in positive or negative ways. These six needs are defined in Tony Robbins' *The Strategic Coaching Handbook* as Certainty, Uncertainty, Love + Connection, Significance, Growth, and Contribution. If you feel a lack of love from a partner or don't feel significant to them, creating arguments is a great way to negatively meet those needs. Think about how important you feel when you are screaming in someone's face – whether they like it or not, in that moment you are connecting.

I would passionately tell G he needed to accept me as I am when I had drunken outbursts. This was the biggest lie of all lies. Why should any other human tolerate me behaving this way? But I felt hopelessly powerless to change.

He decided we should take a break to have some time apart after another blazing drunken row outside his dad's bar, who happened to witness it all. I remember so vividly walking out of his house feeling like my heart had been smashed to pieces. It was 18 months since our love affair had restarted over digestive biscuits and red wine. I didn't see his face again until 13 years later.

Why have I just shared this story? Because until I started to be really honest with myself about what I wanted, what I didn't want, what I was willing to tolerate and what I wasn't, my life was never going to change. Until I truly began to understand why I was operating from this place of complete fear in every relationship, nothing was going to change. How could I live a life on my own terms if I wasn't able to trust my gut, and do the right thing that would help me grow?

If there's one part of you that feels you need to be someone else in order to be accepted, you have lost your way. Living *on purpose* means fully allowing yourself to be you – the unedited, unapologetic best version of you. This doesn't mean accepting the labels you were born with or have been given. It doesn't mean expecting people to accept you when you are operating from a negative mindset. I didn't know how to be that version of me for so long and hated that I projected my own insecurities onto the people I loved, like G.

When you can be confidently *you* in all contexts, that's when you will find true happiness – ditch the posh phone voice, throw off the need to be perfect in front of your employer, and realize you are an adult and don't need to pander to what your parents expect of you. When we hide ourselves, we hide our vulnerabilities, but our vulnerabilities are what connects us all. I am not saying that someone should accept you as you are if you are not a nice person. What I am saying here is that if you cannot be fully honest and open around people that you spend most of your time with, then there is a huge problem.

When I first began dating Rich, I had finally accepted that the common denominator to my failed relationships was **me**. It was at this point I stopped asking partners to accept me as I was and to accept that I needed to go on a journey of healing because I was completely over suffering internally. I allowed myself to be vulnerable enough to seek the help I needed and truly committed to the journey of understanding and developing myself.

Being vulnerable is not a sign of weakness, it's actually completely courageous to stand up and say we are hurting, that we have got it wrong, that somehow, we have lost control of who we are and how we manage life. Being vulnerable is uncomfortable, but if we can embrace stepping into that discomfort to share our truth, we not only have a beautiful opportunity for extreme growth, but also give others permission to be vulnerable too.

We are taught to 'wipe the tears away' and that 'big boys don't cry', so throughout life we adopt ways to protect ourselves from pain. We use defence mechanisms and develop behavioural patterns to ensure we feel safe in the world. Whether we know it or not, we are always just trying to seek security and stability because that's what our Ego craves – as I said before, our brains are designed to keep us safe not happy.

The by-product of doing this is we shut off from creating authentic relationships and we become fixed in the scabs of our childhood past. When we identify why we are wearing the masks, we can begin to heal from the past. This level of self-awareness is the critical component to living a life *on purpose* and leaving the autopilot living behind.

We aren't born with masks; but we learn to put them on thanks to our Ego learning to integrate into society. The great thing is, if we can put them on, we can take them off. Hurrah!

I want to invite you to live your most authentic life, that truly is the first step to being *on purpose*. I invite you to think about these questions:

1 How difficult is it to be yourself around your family, friends and other people?
2 Who do you find it difficult to be yourself around? Why do you think this is true?
3 Where in life do you feel you are wearing masks?
4 If you were to continue to wear a mask, and you were never allowed to really be yourself, what do you think would happen to you over time?

When I started my coaching business, for the first few months that I did videos live on social media I would think carefully about what I said and how I came across. 'I need to be professional' – MASK ALERT! 'I need to swear less – MASK ALERT!' Need is steeped in lack mentality and fear. We are taught so much about what we should be doing in life, that we forget what we need – *which is to be ourselves.*

My business started to expand at a much faster rate when I owned the fact I wasn't perfect. I was too busy to be grammatically correct all the time and I wanted to swear. It puts some people off and it also attracts a whole load of people, and gives them permission to not need to be perfect. Some people will judge me, and others will applaud me and, when we come to terms with the idea that we don't need to be loved or even liked by everyone, we can start to strip away the mask and be comfortable with who we truly are. When we finally learn that trying to please the whole world is impossible, then we can start to actually please ourselves.

In order for you to find your unique purpose on this planet, wouldn't it make sense that you own all parts of you and your uniqueness? Wouldn't it be liberating to stop having to be a chameleon and just be you, unapologetically? One of the decisions I've made that has let me live so *on purpose* that manifestation has become something like second nature is the realization that I don't want to lose myself behind the masks. If I ever feel myself having to mould to someone else's expectation, I remove myself from that situation. The braver you become at showing up as you, the more life will open up to reward your bravery. And once you experience life living as the untamed, unadulterated, unfiltered beautiful you, there is no going back.

28

For the Love of Labels

My head was banging, the room was spinning, and my eyes felt like they were glued together. As I started to piece together what had happened the night before it occurred to me that I was so drunk I'd not taken my contact lenses out and was still fully clothed in last night's outfit.

Against every instinct to want to throw up, I pulled myself up to go and have a shower. As I caught a glimpse of myself in the mirror, I burst out laughing. I had 'COD' written across my forehead in what seemed like permanent fucking marker, which I later found out was courtesy of my housemate Marianna, who thought it would be really funny to see me walk into the kebab shop drunk with COD plastered on my forehead. I now had the joy of walking around with this label on my head for the rest of the day – removing permanent markers off skin takes a few good washings.

COD aside, I had taken on many labels during my life. We forget who the real 'I' is, because we are conditioned to believe that we are our name, our story, our job title, our income, our religion, our colour, our race and our sexual orientation. Labels are what we call ourselves in our head and what others see us as. They are like the hashtags we use to *describe who we are*. It's the totality of these labels that create our identity, our Social Self – our Ego. But these labels are the result of our human experiences – they amount to only a blip in the whole of eternity.

We are so used to identifying with external experiences that create the labels, it takes us away from experiencing who we are on the inside – infinite consciousness having a human experience. The more that we identify with these labels, the more we collectively withdraw from the whole, or the greatest 'I' there is – the I from which we were all created from that big Ocean of Consciousness I talked of earlier.

The more we indulge in our own I, the more we become disconnected from our Soul and from others. We forget that we are all connected, that life isn't a battle of the 'I's', which is why many will spend hours on Facebook having arguments with complete strangers over the labels we have taken on – the common spectacle of Egos fighting Egos. People fighting over sexuality, race, women's rights, politics and so much more. Nothing good vibrationally comes out of this. In fact, this has had horrific consequences on humankind such as wars, terrorism and poverty. Instead of Egos fighting one another for power, Souls could wipe out poverty on this planet within a short space of time. Egos believe we are separated; Souls remember we are connected.

Labels aren't all bad though. If you view yourself as inspiring, hard-working, full of potential, etc., you will be motivated to achieve more to live up to those labels, and since these are positive labels, it will make you feel good about yourself. If you believe you are a winner, you will think like a winner, and this will manifest in the real world.

Of course, the converse inevitably happens with negative labels. Tell a child they are 'slow' or 'naughty' and they will believe that. Negative labels can become self-fulfilling prophecies, which is why I find labelling people with illness one of the most damaging things we can do. The amount of incredible people that I've come across, including myself, who *became* the labels that they had been told by doctors, is extraordinary. I was called a drama queen for as long as I can remember, and you know what – the majority of my teens and twenties were bloody dramatic.

It is our collective job to wake up and try and make this place better for our children, our grandchildren, and every generation that comes after us. Part of that job is understanding we are all the same, whether we like it or not. The more we believe that we are different, the more harm we do to each other. We are like individual unique waves, part of one huge ocean. The tip of each wave may look different, but under the surface we are all connected as a whole. When we can see past the labels, we can see the truth: that pure consciousness is looking through the eyes of those around you; that consciousness just sees life through different perspectives, and we should respect that.

When we choose to see the world through the eyes of Soul, to fully embrace that we are all one, this can bring discomfort because we start to realize how disconnected we have all become from each other and our home planet Earth. Part of living *on purpose* is to allow all those feelings of discomfort to come to the surface, to honour them, to sit with them, and to understand what they are saying.

We need to take the bubble wrap off our hearts and understand that part of living life is to feel the pain that comes when we see we have become disconnected, and to do our bit – to lead with love, not Ego. When you find yourself fighting for your labels, ask yourself why? Fighting for your labels is different than fighting for what truly matters to you. Fighting to prove *you* are right is Ego. Taking a stand for what is right in your heart is different.

We have a choice to give ourselves new labels, to construct a new identity that is rooted in kindness, love and bravery.

You no longer need to define yourself through the label of mental illness or suffering of the past.

You are not tied to the labels you were given as a child that have shaped who you are as an adult.

If a label makes you feel anything less than empowered, if it even slightly feels like it's putting pressure on you as a human, then you have every right to let that label go.

You get to fucking choose who you want to be, and what you wish to live up to, and I sincerely hope you decide to now.

29
Don't Shit in My Vortex

'You are now suspended from working until further notice.'

For the first time in my life, I was utterly speechless as I carried my sorry ass out of the gym I had been an employee at just 15 minutes earlier.

I held back the tears as I walked through the carpark, but when I got in the car I broke down in tears of complete and utter disbelief. *What the fuck just happened?!*

A few months earlier I had proudly secured myself as one of the membership consultants at a gym so that I could make some money during the winter months. I had also decided I wouldn't go back to Club 18–30 (for the third time!) so it made total sense to attempt to grow up and get some sort of 'normal' job in the UK. I was living in Wales now, with my new incredible Welsh boyfriend who was just so utterly divine, that it almost made complete sense to sign up working at a gym on minimum wage, even though now I was the proud owner of a Psychology degree that I had totally winged.

The manager was nothing short of a grade A asshole. He had come out of the army, and he treated us like his soldiers. I'm surprised he didn't have us frog marching into the office and doing 50 burpees in high heels just before potential customers walked in, just for shits and giggles. He induced fear in me, the energy around him was tense and we all felt a pressure to perform.

Oddly enough, I wanted to please him and get in his good books. Note: this was my inner child behaving like this, because as a child I just wanted to be a girl who wanted to please her dad so he didn't get angry. That's the power of the paradigm right there.

I worked hard, and so very nearly had hit my target for the very first time. I was confident I would qualify for the elusive £800 commission. This was a big deal to a 21-year-old, so I asked him if it was possible that since I was so close to my target, if I could I take a Bank Holiday Monday off.

He looked at me as though I'd asked if I could take a dump on his head. He walked over to the board which had our monthly targets set on the first of each month. He crossed out my initial target that was set for me and, as I watched in horror, he took the whiteboard marker and added another ten more sales on to my target. TEN?!

There's absolutely NO way on heaven or earth that I would ever make that by the end of the month. I looked at him in disbelief and said, 'That's unfair!'. His face changed, and he shouted at me to meet him in a different room. In that meeting he suspended me from work with no further notice. I can't even remember what he said as I just sat there in complete and utter mind-blowing disbelief at the series of events of the previous 30 minutes. I just wanted to get out of there as soon as I could.

As you can imagine, what he did was actually completely illegal and his actions made me question the whole of humanity. The label he had of 'boss' took over his every cell and he would not have that threatened. His need to exert power over others was so profound that he would happily break the law rather than be disobeyed or questioned. Of course, I never wanted to step foot back into that office again. I had never fitted in anyway, but here I was again, back to square one thinking, 'What now?'

What I didn't understand then was that all these experiences were shaping me to be the person I am today. I walked out of that gym feeling that this situation had confirmed in me what I had begun to suspect most of my life – that the world was out to get me and that I had pulled the short straw in life where nothing was going to come easy. I went straight back into victim mode – a mode that I had mastered.

I talked about Viktor Frankl earlier – an Austrian psychologist and author of the classic book *Man's Search for Meaning* (1946).

I can assure you that what I was experiencing in my life was nothing compared to what Viktor had been through. He had gone through the gruesome experience of being in Nazi concentration camps in the 1940s and had witnessed the death of everyone he loved. After his horrifying experience in the camps, he developed a theory that it is through a search for meaning and purpose in life that individuals can endure hardship and suffering.

Gosh how I wish someone had given me this wisdom and shift in perspective when I was in my twenties. It never had occurred to my little brain that I had a choice. A choice to protect my energy, and to see things through a different lens. The cold hard truth is, I didn't really ever want to be working at that gym – in fact I found myself feeling tense and uncomfortable every day. I'd often come home crying, but I felt trapped as I needed a job. So, I got a job and I guess at some level, I believed I'd figure out a solution on what would be next. So I was stuck in a perpetual emotional negative state.

What I've come to learn as I've been on this spiritual journey was, in fact, all I was doing by feeling all those vibes and seeing life through a negative lens and allowing myself to be stuck, was shitting in my vortex and I was also cordially inviting everyone else to take a massive shit in it too.

What is the vortex? I hear you say.

The concept of the vortex comes from the teachings of Esther Hicks and the channelled consciousness she calls Abraham. When I first heard that there was a woman who was 'channelling', you could have literally heard my eyes roll. Essentially channelling is communicating with a different dimension or consciousness. When Esther speaks, it isn't actually *her* information she is communicating. Her voice changes, her tone alters and her vocabulary sounds like it is from another era. Whether you believe Esther is the real deal (and millions across the world do), or whether you think she suffers from schizophrenia, or you think she's a fraud, is irrelevant, because once I got over the weirdness of how the information was communicated and started to listen to the message, it changed my life.

Imagine the vortex as a vault that energetically holds everything you have ever had and will ever desire – and the only way into the vault is by using the right code to unlock it. The code however, isn't something you input into the keypad – it's a vibration you give off because the vortex is a sphere of high vibrations only, and when you connect to it, it makes everything possible. A bit like fingerprint recognition, the way into this vault is by being the energetic match to that which you desire. When you do this, you unlock the vault.

This is what I've called 'Tuning Into Universe FM'. Universe FM is the wavelength and energetic stream of abundance and when you dial into that wavelength, you attract abundance. This wavelength is made from the energy of love.

If you think about it, we only ask for things we desire because we think we will **feel better** for having that thing we wish for. You are basically asking for a feeling of harmony, joy, peace and happiness but the paradox is, until you feel those emotions, which in turn affect your vibration, the Law of Attraction won't kick in to make sure you attract what you want. The Law of Attraction states that like attracts like. *You need to be in alignment emotionally with what you desire.* Earlier in the book (Chapter 16) I asked you how it would make you feel when you wrote down the opposite of what you have. This is why.

For example, if you imagine that in a year's time you will have ten times the income you have, or a new amazing partner, think about how that version of you is feeling emotionally and, consequently, vibrating. I will hazard a guess they would be happy! We need to match the vibration of that future self so that like attracts like. You need to become a vibrational master! For you to be in immediate benefit of the vibrational trust fund that is waiting to be signed over to you from the vault, you need to become a vibrational match, but you cannot do that if you are feeling 'less than' or stuck in victim mode which allows your energy to be drained by the external world and the incoming information.

Living *on purpose* involves continual awareness of your own energy and being alert to when your Ego is luring you in to situations that can cause you to end up feeling completely tuned out of Universe FM. When you are a vibrational match, you will also be able to receive information and guidance from that inner wisdom that is there to show you how to bring your desires to fruition.

You cannot be a negative person and expect great things to happen to you.

You cannot expect to be moaning about money all the time and yet trying to win the lottery every week.

That's why aligning your thoughts and your behaviours and actions is crucial for creating You 2.0.

When you are struggling with money, of course your thoughts around money will be, 'Bring me more money, I need more money, I'm struggling so give me money'. But you cannot attract the money you desire when you are vibrationally in alignment with the scarcity and the fact you have no money. *You have got to stop offering contradicting vibrations to your desire.*

Tuning into Universe FM is a *certain state of being and a positive state of mind.* You know you are tuned in because you are feeling good. That means you gotta want what you desire more than you complain, more than you judge, more than you gossip; you gotta want it more than being validated, and more than being right.

If you want to see what 'being right' looks like, just head over onto Facebook or Twitter and type in COVID-19 conspiracy or vaccinations. You will see threads of people fighting for their right to be right. Why? Because they would rather be right than happy. I'd rather be sitting in my vortex, with a million pounds in my bank account, eating dinner from my new dining room in my dream house, taking holidays five times a year and being at peace than being right and fighting with the rest of the world's egos. That doesn't mean not standing up for what you care about to make a difference, it means standing back from arguing with people that results in you feeling frustrated and deflated.

Becoming acutely aware of your thoughts takes discipline, but it's paramount to your success of becoming vibrationally aligned.

When I was on my perpetual hunt for Mr Right, the number of times I must have thought and said things like:

- 'He doesn't exist'
- 'I'm cursed'
- 'There are no good guys.'

Inside the vortex, my future husband was there waiting, with his thick Yorkshire accent, blue eyes and cute stutter. He was there all along, but I was vibrating at the wrong frequency for him to waltz into my life. If you are trying to find the love of your life, know that they are there waiting for you – but right at that moment you just aren't where your lover is. Your lover is in love with *you inside of the vortex* and they will wait for you as long as is necessary, until you show up to the vibrational party!

When you tune in:

- You are talking about what you *do* want, not what you *don't* want
- You love to praise people instead of criticize
- You love to joke rather than judge
- You choose to be optimistic over being pessimistic
- You choose to see life through the lens of Soul not Ego, which means choosing to see the good and act through love.

Soul after all is the heart of your Spiritual Self, and the heart is the place where you give love from.

The key point here is you get to choose. The choice to master your thoughts and vibrations takes discipline but it's a practice that becomes easier and more natural with time – and a practice that will shift your energy and trajectory of your life forever.

30
Pivot Your Perspective

One of the things that I love teaching my students is a concept I like to call Pivoting your Perspective – something we'll explore in more detail shortly.

The incredible late Dr Wayne Dyer teaches us that every situation is emotionally neutral and the only thing that adds emotion to it **is us**. We add emotions by the way we perceive situations and give meaning to them. This is why Viktor Frankl's work is so profound. Despite the adversity, he chose to see things differently.

Instead of walking out of that gym job with gratitude that the Universe had just saved me from having to spend one more minute working in that god awful place – which by the way it totally was – I chose to see things through a negative lens and made it about me as a person. I internalized the experience and gave it a meaning: *'Something is wrong with me'*. Yes, at a surface level, I know there was something gravely wrong with my boss, but when I peeled back the layers, I believed it was **me** that was the problem and that everything was always against me.

Frankl believed that we are all motivated by something called a 'will to meaning', which basically means 'a desire to find meaning in life'. He argued that life can have meaning even in the most miserable of circumstances and that the motivation for living comes from finding that positive meaning. We can call that 'finding the silver lining' (or in my case the pink one!). It's a choice to find positive meaning in every situation despite the fact it may have choke-slammed the shit out of you.

The truth is I chose to find gratitude and meaning when my then eight-year-old brother got diagnosed with leukaemia. I chose to see the beautiful moments that came out of the fear of the reality that his survival rates were slim.

Moments such as my mother going to the hospital to see her ex-husband, after having not talked to him for 15 years, to give him a hug and offer her support as he battled with the news his son had cancer.

It changed my dad's whole perspective in life and caused him to re-evaluate everything. Our relationship grew stronger and closer through that adversity, a gift that I could have never imagined.

It led me to understanding more about cancer and nutrition and healing alternatives, which helped my brother go into full remission in just six months, despite the doctors telling us he would be on chemo for four years.

We prayed hard for his recovery, but never once did I wish it didn't happen because it brought us together in a way that only adversity could and prepared us for another life-changing family event that would come to us years later.

> 'Everything can be taken from a man but one thing: the last of the human freedoms – to choose one's attitude in any given set of circumstances, to choose one's own way.'
>
> *Viktor Frankl*

People can try to break you down, but your choice to give what meaning you want to it is one thing that no other single body on this planet can ever take away from you. Find that gratitude, find that peace, find the goddamn silver lining, even if it kills you.

Most people will not go for their big hairy scary dreams because they have this sense that others will judge them, We honestly feel like people are waiting on the sidelines ready to gossip, ready to pick out how we are getting it wrong and ready to toast when we fall flat on our fucking faces. Paranoia can be defined as unjustified suspicion and mistrust of other people. I know that this was one of the reasons it took me so long to set up my coaching business.

The reason we feel that others are judging us is because they are and – let's be frank here – you do it too, all day long without realizing. People will judge you for staying in a job you don't like, but then will judge you for flying the nest and trying to set up your own thing. They will judge you for being too fat, too thin, too loud, too quiet, and [fill in the blanks].

We will never get it right if we are trying to please the rest of the world, so surely it's insanity to even try. We might as well decide what we want and at least we can please ourselves. Which is why the concept of being an inverse paranoid was so liberating to me.

Instead of worrying that everyone is out to get me, I started to believe and think that everyone was out to support me.

Imagine that everyone is waiting with pom poms and prosecco to toast your success.

Imagine that everyone truly supports your every decision.

Imagine that everything that comes into your life comes into your life for the sole purpose of helping you grow into the best fucking version of yourself.

Decide that every person that enters your life is here to teach you a valuable lesson that your Soul needs for you to manifest your best life.

How different would your life look if you could think like that? How different would you feel?

Often, we hold onto really traumatic experiences as a child and we find it hard to forgive the person who hurt us. I want to offer you up a coaching tool that I use with my clients for pivoting their perspective on it. When someone causes us emotional hurt, the first thing we do is assume it's about us. We do not have the mental faculties to see past what is happening in that moment and consequently we make decisions that then create beliefs about it.

Let me use Sophie as an example. Sophie endured watching her mum being dragged across the floor and kicked and punched as a three-year-old. No child should ever have to experience this horror. She was then herself in hospital with a cracked skull because her dad pushed her. Sophie was angry with her father, rightly so, for her whole life especially as the police never did anything and he got away with it (don't even get me started on that system!). As a three-year-old, Sophie had a core belief that, 'People who love us will hurt us'.

How do you think that belief played out in Sophie's life? By the age of 31, she had been in several physically abusive relationships, because this is what Sophie was unconsciously programmed to believe was normal and it confirmed her belief that those that love us will hurt us. As I worked with Sophie deeply in a state of hypnosis, one of the things I asked her to do was to see her dad as a little boy and ask him why he caused her so much pain. What she came to realize was that he was a product of his own abuse and that, while it was completely unacceptable, when she could see it from a different perspective, she could start to let go of the anger that had a stronghold on her life.

Sophie had been suffering with gut problems for many years. Research has shown that some short- and long-term health problems, including digestion problems, are linked to unmanaged anger. When we hold onto grievances with other people, and refuse to forgive them, the only person that suffers is ourselves. My job as Sophie's coach was to help her see things in a different way, because the stuck thought patterns were keeping her in a negative state and causing physical problems. As children we don't have the capacity to rationalize and see that it isn't about us, and that people who hurt us are acting in that way because of their own pain.

As Buddha said, staying angry is like drinking poison out of your own cup. Forgiveness is the highest act of bravery in my eyes. Forgiveness does not tell the person who has hurt you that you accept or understand what they have done. Forgiveness is a choice to take back the power you have given to them. It's a powerful decision to choose your own happiness in the present, rather than hold onto the pain of the past.

Happy people don't hurt other people.

Successful people don't troll people.

Peaceful people don't project their shit on others.

When we forgive, we are not saying that what they did was right, what we are saying is 'I no longer allow the anger you have caused to sit there like a turd in my vortex'.

31
Bad Feelings

'Mummy, when I listen to these people talk, it gives me bad feelings,' Layla-Rose said sadly.

My daughter was only eight years old and I was so in driving mode, trying to get to her friend's birthday party on time, that I'd momentarily forgotten to switch the radio channel over before the news came on.

'I know baby, the news is never nice, which is why you don't ever need to listen to it.'

'All they keep saying is how bad everything is. Surely that makes everyone sad? So it's best that no one listens to it. Otherwise, they will never want to leave their house,' she went on to say.

Sometimes we underestimate the sheer profound wisdom that comes out of a child's mouth. If only children were allowed to make the decision about what to broadcast on the news. Richard and I made a decision to protect our children from listening to the news because of this exact reason.

'If you take a gorgeous orange and squeeze it hard, what comes out of it?' I asked Layla.

'Orange juice obviously!?'

'What we put inside of us, is what will come out sweetheart. If we listen to things that give us bad feelings and make us scared of the world, then when the world comes to squeeze us or put pressure us, bad feelings come out. If we listen to positive things that make us feel happy, what do you think will come out?'

'Good feelings!' she replied.

If we are being fed fear, then under pressure, fear will come out. If we allow only positive energy and messaging to enter us, when we are under pressure, we are more likely to be able to deal with

it in a positive way. It's part of your purpose to have an awareness of what you are allowing into your world and consequently
affecting your vibrational well-being, because this after all is the
key to transforming your life. We need to become aware of all that
potentially shitting in our vortex.

If I squeezed you, what would come out of you?

Living *on purpose* means leading with the awareness of another
of the Universal Laws – the Law of Cause and Effect. Every
thought and action has to have an effect. There is no effect without a cause. What I just freaking adore about teaching manifestation is that it forces you to truly think about how you are showing
up in the world for yourself and others. It forces you to think
about what will come out of you in any given situation. Will it be
anger or happiness, positivity or negativity?

Do you think it's by some glorious accident that in order for
you to be able to create the life you want, you simply need to
think great thoughts and feel good? To remember we are connected to everyone and everything and to choose to treat other
humans with the love and kindness you would want to receive.
It's so simple.

So if it's that simple, you may be wondering why it feels so
hard? Why are so many people suffering? We have an in-built success mechanism – so why the heck do so many of us feel like we
are failing?

What if I told you that we live in a world where we *aren't
supposed to know* how powerful we are, a world where we are
taught to react to external circumstance and a world where we
are indoctrinated into a false sense of self, so that we literally cannot help but to live through the lens of Ego and fear, instead of
Soul and peace? What if I said – and don't get the men in white
jackets to take me away before you've heard me out – that we
are being slowly manipulated to perceive the world in a certain
way because that keeps the majority as good little humanoids that
don't create wildly abundant success? What if the powers above
us know that we are powerful and yet don't want us to know,

which is why mindset and manifestation work aren't part of the curriculum?!

I've been taught well by my dad, who is a lawyer, to not just put forward ideas but to back them up with evidence. This is what is so wrong with social media – people will fight for a view and they don't even know why they are fighting for it and cannot back it up with evidence! They don't even realize how absurd it is that they are fighting about something that they've never ever studied in their life.

I was absolutely shocked to find an official document on the CIA website for US Military Intelligence where a commander of the military was asked to investigate human consciousness. Back in 1983, they were looking at the Gateway Process and whether it was possible for humans to transcend different dimensions. The whole thing blew my mind, but a piece of it that left my jaw open is that this official document reported something called Patterning. In this document it clearly says:

> 'This technique involves the use of consciousness to achieve desired objectives in the physical, emotional and intellectual sphere. It involves concentration on the desired objective in a Focus 12 state, an extension of an individual's perception of the objective into the whole expanded consciousness, and its projection into the universe with the intention that the desired objective is already a matter of established achievement which is destined to be realized within the time frame specified. This particular methodology is based on the belief that thought patterns generated by our Consciousness in a state of expanded awareness create Holograms which represent the situation we desire to bring about, and in doing so, establish the basis for actual realization of the goal.'

Say whaaat?! This document was teaching the military how to manifest? So, if the CIA knew we had the power to change our lives, then why weren't they shouting this from the rooftops? Well, the same CIA also conducted an illegal study on how humans could be brainwashed. Look, I don't mean to sound cynical, but I smell a rat.

When it comes to living *on purpose* and finding our unique purpose, we need to truly see what is going into us mentally, emotionally and spiritually, so that we can see what is coming out of us vibrationally. We need to become conscious about everything we consume, from the food we eat, to the information we listen to, to the conversations we have with people because every moment has an impact on your vibrational health, which is either helping you thrive or keeping you stuck and unwell.

Adverts

Let's start with good old advertising. Think about when you watch adverts on TV – what is the purpose of it? Well those companies pay thousands, maybe even millions, to get the best people to create adverts that psychologically manipulate someone to purchase. To make us feel like we need what someone is selling. They hire people that understand how to use our own faculties against us. Adverts succeed in making us feel inadequate until we buy the new lip plumping lipstick or cock enlarging pill that is being advertised, and the fact it is operating on the deepest level of human response makes it oh-so more powerful. We cannot escape advertising, it's all around us on TV, on radio and on that newsfeed.

Television

A series of experiments conducted by psychologist Herbert E. Krugman in the 1970s revealed that, when we watch television, within just 30 seconds our brain activity switches from the left to the right hemisphere. The left hemisphere is where we logically think about things, in contrast to the right side which treats incoming data uncritically, leading to *emotional, rather than logical responses.*

Why is this relevant to you?

Well this shift from left to right brain activity also causes the release of endorphins, thus, it is actually possible to become physically addicted to watching television, and when people become addicted then it provides an opportunity for using TV as a way to distort our perceptions of reality and, of course, for advertisers to get to us. Watching television also causes activity in some brain regions (such as the neocortex) to diminish, and other regions (such as the limbic system) to increase. The latter is part of the lower brain region, which is associated with more primitive mental functions, such as the 'fight or flight' response, and is commonly referred to as the reptilian brain.

The reptilian brain makes it possible for us to survive as human beings, but this can leave us exposed to the manipulations of television programmers. Television perpetuates awful and incorrect stereotypes such as Black people being criminals, Middle Eastern people being terrorists, the world as being unsafe – it can create fears that we wouldn't have had before, such as fears of sharks or spiders. The reptilian brain is unable to distinguish between reality and the simulated reality of television. On a conscious level we may think something is 'only a film', but our brain sees it as real and our body reacts accordingly. I remember crying, holding onto the edge of my seat, while watching *Titanic*, praying that Rose would find Jack – and I'm sure you have experienced something similar. Your body goes into stress and starts releasing cortisol, which over time can cause you to become unwell.

Whilst this is of course not the case for many entertainment shows, if there was in fact someone trying to programme our perception of the world, wouldn't it be smart to use something like a TV, which almost every household has. This is of course only one medium that can be used to manipulate our perceptions. And if you think this is far-fetched then Google 'Project MKUltra' and you will see that mind control is not something new and this is exactly what was done by the CIA.

'The conscious and intelligent manipulation of the organized
habits and opinions of the masses is an important element in
democratic society. Those who manipulate this unseen mechanism
of society constitute an invisible government which is the true
ruling power of our country.'

Edward Bernays

News

What percentage of the news is sharing positivity? Is it possible
to fathom that the news is reported in such a way to keep us in
a state of fear, a mindset of scarcity and stop us from living our
full potential? This doesn't mean everything put out there has this
purpose but a feature in the American Psychology Association
shows exactly the effect the media has on creating fear and the
impact that has on us as humans.

A 2015 study referred to the Ebola outbreak, and while there
were just ten confirmed US cases (all of them people who had
direct contact with Ebola patients) parents proceeded to pull their
kids out of school. Whilst the spread of Ebola was understandably
a shock, psychologists were not surprised by how the fears were
inflated in comparison to the risk.

For decades, psychologists such as Paul Slovic have studied how
humans perceive risk and what causes so many people to overreact to epidemics, terrorist attacks and other extreme events, even
when their personal risk is infinitesimal. Yes, and here's the kicker
to their findings, those same people are less threatened by diseases
that are far more likely to harm them, such as the flu.

Slovic said, 'The minute the Ebola threat was communicated, it
hit all of the hot buttons: it can be fatal, it's invisible and hard to
protect against, exposure is involuntary and it's not clear that the
authorities are in control of the situation.' It seems to me, and I
witnessed this myself as I saw people scream at each other in the
middle of Tesco over face masks during COVID, that people start

to lose their ability to think rationally because the fear becomes so pervasive when it surrounds us every day.

Barbara Reynolds, a psychologist and director of the Division of Public Affairs at the Centers for Disease Control and Prevention (CDC) says, 'Modern communication allows people to have a more intimate experience with a threat that's not real.' And thanks to hyperbolic media plastering a threat on every news channel multiple times a day, people begin to see a threat. 'American media have the propensity to find – and publicize – aberrant behavior, helping to perpetuate a myth that people tend to respond to a crisis with panic.'

The media has a paramount effect on our mindset and how we perceive the world and, with the news on multiple times day through different mediums, we are exposing ourselves to negative stories on repeat. And remember how our subconscious mind works - it learns through repetition.

The Nudge Unit was established in the Cabinet Office in 2010 by David Cameron's government to apply behavioural science to public policy operations across the world. It is called 'nudge' after the book by Richard Thaler (who went on to win the Nobel Prize in Economics) and Cass Sunstein, which sets out how people can be influenced by 'choice architecture' into making better choices in their own interests. In short, the government even hires people to nudge us into behaving in certain ways using behavioural science. The greatest minds know how we innately react as humans – we are simple creatures after all and they will use that to help us 'make better choices' – which they claim is for our own good. *But is this truly the case?*

This is just a needle in a haystack of evidence and studies showing that, without ever realizing, we are fed information that alters our perception of life every day. At any given moment we can be exposed to multiple shits in our vortex.

We think we are making our own decisions about our life, but it's paramount that you start to understand WHY you have made those decisions and to see the effect of those thoughts.

For you to live in vibrational alignment with your dream life and transform your life, you need to become aware so you at least have the choice and conscious awareness over what information your brain is decoding.

What goes in, will come out.

Every cause has an effect.

Never ever in history has the news anchor come on and said 'Good morning, what a bloody wonderful day today, no one has bombed anyone, no one has been murdered and, in fact, a leprechaun was sighted helping an old woman cross the road. It is just a wonderful day to be a human.'

I chose to give up listening and watching mainstream media about seven years ago. It does not mean that I am not aware of what is going on in the world, but I now have an understanding of how we are being made to think and feel, and I for one would rather think for myself!

I am so ashamed to even admit this, but after 9/11, I remember on the first plane I got on I saw a woman in a hijab and, for a momentary second, I was scared. I come from a Muslim family, so can you imagine how much fear was put into my world then? That even the look of a hijab on a plane could cause me to momentarily think I was in danger. My brain had collated information based on what was going on in the world from watching every second of news and it was pulling up that information to signal to me there might be danger. I was only a teenage girl at the time and felt utterly ashamed that this thought had even entered my mind. However, this is the power of the media.

If you take time to look, you will see we are fed stories that we are not good enough so we must buy XYZ and do XYZ. We are led to fear the world so that we keep safe and small. Until you become conscious of this, you will always stay trapped within a mental prison created by fear that you aren't even aware is there, because it's become so normal.

Locked into the matrix of a small perception of the world, we are not encouraged to break free of our limitations and of the status quo – we stay small and dumbed down. But who would want us to feel this way? Always follow the money trail. There isn't money to be made in healthy, happy people.

I am telling you this because I care. I care about the world my children are growing up in. And you should care too. I want you to take ownership for your health, your wealth, your relationships and your life. The simplest way to protect your energy – so you can stay turned on, tuned in, and tapped in the flow of abundance – is firstly to monitor what you are consuming and become aware of how it makes you feel.

Stop spending time with people who bring your vibe down. We have all been around energy vampires – the type of people who suck the life out of us by their mere presence. As you start to transcend humanoid consciousness and start to see things in a different light, you will begin to witness more than ever the people that spend all day complaining, blaming, criticizing, nagging and moaning. You will be in an elite class of humans who can spot when someone is trying to push the buttons of your Ego and get a reaction, and you will be able to simply walk away because you *know* that you are pushing your desires away by engaging in the riff raff.

Consume good food to keep your body healthy and consume good information to keep your mind strong.

Be curious and question everything.

Do your own research and don't always accept the mainstream narrative.

Protect your vessel of energy as though your life depends on it – because it does.

32
Surrender

'Love will find you when you least expect it.'

Lets' talk about this saying...

I spent most of my twenties parading across the Mediterranean hoping that I would find Mr Right. But, what if I didn't want love to find me when I was least expecting it? What if I was throwing up after a dodgy kebab, or it was the time of the month and I was feeling bloated and grumpy – I didn't want love to find me then. I needed love to find me when my skin was clear, my hair was blow dried and I felt fabulous.

But the kicker is, the more you worry about the absence of what you desire, that energy will push what you want further away.

It was on Thursday 15 July 2010 that I mentally declared that I was going to be single and actually enjoy it. I had been in another 18-month relationship, this time with a boy from Australia. When he broke up with me I cried, but my tears were of relief. We were not right for each other, we had never been, but I could never seem to walk away. When he made the decision, it felt like someone had cut the toxic cord that had joined us.

I made a decision. I was going to travel again. I was going to enjoy the rest of the summer with full gusto. I was 24, single and in Ibiza. I admired girls who were able to sleep with guys and not fall in love with them after day one – it was a curse I had and I was ready to break it. I was going to have fun! For once in my life I decided I didn't want to be in a relationship and it was time to find myself. I didn't even know what that meant, but a great place that evening to start was to go out, drink and dance the night away at Eden nightclub. I let go, I surrendered, and my desire to find the love of my life was parked.

Do you know what happened?

On Friday 16 July, 24 hours later, while minding my own single-life business, I met this really cute Yorkshire boy, with tanned skin, bright blue eyes and a lisp I managed to pick up on despite the fact the music was pumping. He gave me butterflies and while a gaggle of girls always seemed to be surrounding him, he seemed to gravitate towards me. We laughed on the bar crawls, we danced on the booze cruise, and on Tuesday 20 July, his last night on holiday, I thought he would be the first guy I would test out my new 'will shag you 'cause I like you and will not fall in love with you and will forget about you the next day' method (sorry mum).

Well, the method didn't quite work out how I'd planned.

The gorgeous, funny, chilled boy from Yorkshire was called Richard Hibbert and I didn't know at that moment, that after that night, I'd never sleep with another man again.

When you let go of trying to manipulate the outcome, the universal flow of abundance with everything you want can flow straight to you. The Universe knows what you want. Good heavens I'd spent enough days daydreaming about marriage and kids while listening to 'My Heart Will Go On' by Céline Dion, that it was etched on the universal mind in permanent marker never to be removed for the whole of eternity.

Richard and I have been together 11 years, have three beautiful girls and one on the way, and I can assure you that, while our love story was not all glitter and unicorns, there was a connection I had with him that I had never felt in my life and I finally knew what it felt like to be completely in love with someone and be able to be completely myself.

There is something very counterproductive in doing, doing, doing and trying, trying, trying, so, so, so hard – because you are a human being, not a human doing and when we can BE, then we can have and do everything we want. Let that sink in. When you BE the energy of love, happiness, gratitude and joy, you can have what you want and do what you please. When you walk away from desperation, need, and a wanting rooted in fear, you attract what you desire ten times quicker.

By fully accepting the situation and completely and utterly committing to the moment, and enjoying the moment, I was now in the right state of being to attract what I wanted. Can you see now why you perhaps have been repelling what you desire instead of attracting it?

So many people are looking for the results and are tense and determined about the manifestation of their desires. Your work is to trust that, if you let go, you will float downstream on the river of abundance towards what you desire. Whenever you feel stressed out about the thing you want, you need to make peace with exactly where you are. When you do that, you feel the tension leave your body, and boom you are an open channel for that which you want to flow straight to you.

'Eat, Pray, Love + Dance Like No-one is fucking Watching.'

So as you can see, living *on purpose* is a choice.

A choice to choose love over fear.

To choose a better thought and a better perspective.

A choice to decide what you want and to commit to using your imagination faculties to create inside of the fourth dimension.

A choice to unapologetically be you, to take off the masks, to leave your labels at the door.

A choice to flow through life, to stop caring what others are thinking of you.

A choice to recognize that there is more than your brain will ever logically be able to understand and that is ok.

A choice to close your eyes, silence your mind so that it doesn't run the show.

A choice to surrender, to be, and allow the Universe to do its thing.

You have and always will have a choice. So don't throw that choice away, because your dreams are depending on it.

PART THREE
Your Purpose

33
Unstuck Yourself

'You were born with potential. You were born with goodness and trust. You were born with ideals and dreams. You were born with greatness. You were born with wings. You are not meant for crawling, so don't. You have wings. Learn to use them and fly.'

Rumi

Let's get one thing clear from the get-go: we are multidimensional humans with many purposes in life, and trying to limit ourselves to just one would be like trying to commit to one flavour of ice-cream for the rest of our life. It would be a travesty.

My purpose is, in equal amounts, to be a mother as it is to help others to master their mindset so they can transform their lives. My purpose when I was 24 is different from my purpose now at 35, and my purpose now may evolve and change by the time I'm 50.

We can find meaning in life from many different things, at different times, and it's our job to be open to this fluidity. The Ocean of Consciousness is fluid and you are part of it. Thinking that you only have one purpose is limited and, if I've taught you anything by this point, it's to not try to box your thinking into a tiny Tiffany ring box.

Think about an acorn. An acorn reaches its fullest potential when it becomes an oak tree. It's blueprinted for that *exact outcome*. You also, my dear, are blueprinted with your fullest potential, and the map to the highest manifestation of yourself lies within the dreams you have! Those big ass dreams are your blueprint. They are your fullest potential.

Annoyingly, acorns have an unfair advantage over humans. They don't have an Ego, so an acorn isn't going to be busy wondering if the maple tree is going to go for cheeky prosecco with the mulberry bush (and bitch about it behind its back) if it decides to reach its full potential of being an oak tree. It just becomes it – without resistance, with full unapologetic knowingness that it's destined to be a majestic oak.

But, sadly, one of the greatest human afflictions is we care so much about what people that don't even matter to us think about us. We would rather stay a small acorn than worry about someone judging us for blossoming into a mighty oak. But, isn't that just incredibly ridiculous?

We say things like 'Maybe in another life...' when that crazy idea springs into our mind. *As if we have another life!* As if this is the dress rehearsal! You are on the stage my darling, and whether you hide behind the curtains or stand right in the spotlight, the show will surely go on.

The problem with hiding behind the curtains of your life is that you feel an electric restlessness in your body, it will bubble under your skin constantly letting you know that you are stuck. When we allow the external world to stop us from growing internally, it causes literal discomfort in our physical self.

When I was eight, I decided it was completely sensible to take superglue out of my dad's huge brown leather desk to fix a broken part of my Sylvanian family. 'Never ever use this alone' he had warned, but as an innocent eight-year-old who had never experienced the wrath of misused superglue, I thought I would be ok. Of course, the glue went everywhere, and I was left in utter fear as I realized that my fingers were stuck together.

Panic rose over me as the fumes entered every part of my nose. I broke the rules and now this was my punishment. I envisaged paramedics having to pry my fingers apart while my parents scolded me for being so stupid. What if I would never be able to write again?! I genuinely thought I would forever be the girl who had her fingers stuck together.

However stuck you may feel, you are not physically glued to anything or anywhere. The only thing stuck is your thoughts. Your thoughts are firmly attached to an old paradigm that isn't serving you, and it's time to pry yourself apart, like my nanny successfully managed to do with my fingers.

You have the choice to let go of old thinking, step out of the mental cage that has kept you from living your fullest potential and be brave enough to see the bigger version of yourself and your life. When you allow yourself to see that your desires are your roadmap, and that roadmap has been specifically designed for you, there is nothing to be scared of. Your dreams were made for you, because they are possible to manifest.

So, step out from behind the curtain and say 'Here I fucking am!'

34
What Do You Want to Do When You Grow Up?

I heard this question several times from the age of four till I was 29. Because I hadn't actually found that elusive *one* thing I was *meant to do* when I was a fully grown adult. Through the lack of clarity, there was however one constant thread in my life – I knew I wanted to help people, and until I could find a more sensible way of doing it, I helped raucous twenty-somethings have the best holidays by selling them booze cruises and foam parties for six years. I loved the feeling when someone thanked me for making an impact on their life – even if that involved a week-long hangover.

We all have something special to offer the world and trying to figure that out as a child, before we have even had a chance to really experience life, feels counterintuitive to me. Also, add the pressure that we are taught to only choose one thing, and suddenly we are fluid, vast, limitless oceans of consciousness having to choose tiny buckets to live in for the rest of life.

You are a unique expression of universal energy; it doesn't matter who you are, where you live, what race you are, or what your experience is – you have multiple things to offer that *only you can deliver in your own unique way*. But we need to connect back to ourselves in order to remember this.

You have a *dharma*, which translates from Sanskrit as a 'unique gift' or 'special talent'. And being able to lick your elbow doesn't count my friend! The ancient texts suggest that when we can blend our unique talent with helping others in the world, this is the sweet spot of creating unlimited abundance in not only happiness, but also wealth. However, this also involves thinking outside of the small box that society tries to put us in and following our intuition. You may be thinking as you read these words, 'How do I find my *dharma*, Noor?!'. Well, firstly you stop trying to find it. You have never lost it, you just haven't stayed quiet enough or become aware enough to see the keys in your hands. You haven't been tuned into the right wavelength to receive the intel on your purpose.

Let's say you are trying to listen to old school garage music (my fave!) on the radio, but you tune into a completely different radio station (frequency) and you land on talkSPORT. I can guarantee you that even with all the wishing in the world, you will be stuck listening to a bunch of blokes talking about grown men who kick balls. There will categorically be no garage music incoming. This is what happens to us all day long. We are dialled into the wrong freaking radio station and wondering why we are being subjected to boring talk about football, instead of dancing in delight. Our purpose is our music. Our purpose makes us want to dance in life. When we are too busy to tune in, we will be stuck listening to old men talk shit for the rest of our lives. When we tune in, purpose finds us.

Back in 2014, my purpose found me. I was sitting by the pool in Bali reading a book on sales. I was in a job I didn't like but I truly had no clue what I wanted to do. I would dread waking up in the morning and would watch the clock all day, counting down each agonizing minute till I could get back home to my daughter. I had started to dip my toes into self-development and was intently listening to Jim Rohn in my car. He taught me one of the most valuable lessons that shaped who I became. He insisted that in order to change my life, I needed to show up every day with presence, great intention and joy, despite the fact I was not happy with my external circumstances. I had nothing to lose and no other options, so instead of dreading each day, I decided to become really, really good at my job, to embrace each day, to try to enjoy it. And thus, I was sitting by the pool reading a book on sales on my honeymoon – making a commitment to show up every day with the aspiration and motivation to succeed and become the best at my current role and make as much commission as possible.

Little did I know as I basked in that Bali sun, devouring each sentence, that this book was written by a sales coach. As I read how he travelled the world teaching others and coaching them to be salespeople, it felt like a bolt of spiritual electricity zoomed and coursed through every cell in my body. I literally remember every hair on my body standing on edge as though I'd stepped into an ice cold room, instead of being sat in the glorious Balinese sunshine.

I knew in that moment I wanted to be a coach. I wanted to teach people at live events.

From that very moment, sitting by that pool in Bali, the whole trajectory of my life changed in an instant. Purpose found me because I chose to be tuned in. Instead of staying in victim mode, feeling helpless and wishing my day away - I shifted my energy and by doing that I opened the floodgates for purpose to find me. When you start to elevate your awareness and consciousness and operate from a place of Soul lead by joy, not Ego lead by fear, you will see that everything you seek will begin to seek you.

Right now, you are most probably tuned into completely the wrong frequency for your purpose to find you. The route to purpose making itself known to you rests upon you being able to also listen to those internal nudges and gut feelings. When we tune into Universe FM, we recognize that inspiration is direct communication from something bigger and we learn to have courage in taking action to make it happen. We become open to reaching our full potential, we begin to trust the ideas that come to us.

But a great starting point is to look for what matters to you.

Look at what you are good at.

Find out how you can become better at it.

Find out how you can help others with it.

You have something to offer because you have a dharma. We all do.

Your job is to create the mental space to explore what that is and then to follow the divine instruction to make shit happen.

35
Clues

'So give me a bug and a jumping flea. Give me two snails and
lizards three.'

I recited each word proudly to the examiner who was staring at
me with a smile. I had already recited a poem about cats, and I
was now nervously yet confidently performing an excerpt from
George's Marvellous Medicine.

I was just nine years old, standing in an empty school hall on
Saturday in the middle of taking my speech and drama exam. At
school I was average at most things, and never knew what it felt
like to excel at anything. However, my teachers always picked me
to be the narrator in school plays and urged my mum to send me
to speech and drama as this was clearly a natural talent of mine.
I'll never forget the day I received my certificate for that exam – I
beamed with joy at seeing the word 'Honours'. Honours was the
highest, there was no higher to go – this is what it felt like to excel
at something! That is one of my first memories of thinking I was
really good at something.

I am a natural communicator, so it is no surprise to my parents
that I love to hold live events, speak on stage and communicate
messages via live videos to others in my career now. As a child
I'd spend my pocket money on buying *The Stage* – a newspaper
dedicated to sharing theatre news. I'd skip straight to the back of
the huge broadsheet where it said 'Jobs and Auditions' and I'd lose
myself in the daydream that I'd be snapped up for a main part on
a West End show. My parents never actually took me to any, but
the daydream seemed to satiate my desire.

My love for performance did not manifest in a part in Les Mis, but as an adult it's even better than I could ever have dreamed of. Hosting live and online events, teaching people across the globe on video and allowing my creativity to flow through social media content, has given my inner child a way to perform. The best part is, I don't need to act. I get to be ME and help people along the way.

On top of singing and dancing, as a child I spent hours writing stories and poems (author in the making), my teachers called me a chatterbox (great communicator), bossy (great leader) and I was always thinking of ways to make money by doing sales in front of my house (entrepreneur in the making). Finally, I loved being chief advice giver and helping people (coach).

Take a moment to go back to when you were a child. I want you to close your eyes and imagine yourself peeling back the years, the months, the weeks, the days to when you were a child. Our childhood can leave valuable clues about our purpose and how to live *on purpose*. Adults that have suppressed the creativity they loved as a child often find themselves feeling 'off'.

What did you love doing?

What made you happy?

What were things that you were naturally good at?

What did people praise you for?

What clues does your childhood hold?

Some of you may struggle to remember, so ask your parents if they are around or other family members. It's super fun to see what they say about you.

In addition to searching your childhood for clues, I want you to think about all the valuable knowledge and skills you have gained throughout your working life. Besides the fact I was able to drink a pint upside down (thank you Club 18–30 bar crawl challenge), my years working abroad had taught me to become a better public speaker, motivated me to work for myself (as it was target driven), and taught me how to work when sleep deprived, which prepared me for motherhood like a treat!

In terms of skills, I've learned so much about the online world over the last six years and have developed those skills to become better. As someone who had never really won anything at school, for the first time in life, when I was a holiday rep, I got noticed for being good at something and even have six shiny trophies which I collected over those years to show for it. I was continually the top seller, my team won awards and this gave me a sense of fulfilment.

What skills will you have picked up through life that are now in your toolbox? Grab a paper and list all of them.

Many of us have the ingredients for serving others right under our noses, but we don't realize it because we are so busy thinking we aren't good enough. Yes, you may not have abilities that no one else has, because humans possess the same biological machinery, but *you* are what makes that ability unique. There's more coaches in the world than I've had hot dinners, but there's only one me.

36
You Have a Million Pounds
Inside of You

Something I learned that helped me create the most abundance in my life is the idea that we each have a million pounds of value inside of us. No, it's not stashed in notes right between your ribs and cushioned neatly around your organs, but energetically it is there, ready to be withdrawn. We all have the faculties, creativity and ability to create any income that we desire. You may not desire to make a million pounds, but whatever it is you desire – you have the ability to create. Remember, a desire is only yours if it's possible for you.

Take a moment to think about what money really is. Physically it can be just paper with a number printed on it or a piece of copper or nickel. Or it is a number you see on the screen of your online banking. Money is used as a medium of exchange and is a representation of the value we give to the world. Someone will pay more (a.k.a. exchange energy) for something they deem more valuable. A pay scale in the job world is created based on how valuable someone is to an employer and also to the world.

The reason jobs pay minimum wage is because the system has decided that 'anyone' could technically do those jobs. Those employees aren't considered as valuable as those doing more specialist jobs. Of course we are all valuable human beings but this is how the system labels us. If you're a doctor you are considered more valuable as it's taken seven years of education and, therefore, the salary reflects that value and you will get more numbers moved across a computer screen into your bank account, which are still just numbers on a computer screen that represents the value.

Society and employers decide what the value of a job is, but if you can find ways to be of service to others and offer them more value, then nothing is stopping you from offering more value and thus having the numbers on your bank account screen to reflect that. Each and every one of us has the ability to become more valuable, it's a choice. The only person stopping you from increasing your personal worth to the world, is you. In fact, it is our birth right to create all the abundance we desire, but we need to figure out how we offer a million pounds worth of value. For example, you could offer a million people something that is of only one pound or dollar value or find something that 100 people would exchange ten thousand pounds for. There is always a problem that needs solving and always humans that need serving. There will be people that gravitate towards *you* and *you only* for the solution you offer, whether that is in a job or in your own business. Of course, working in a job has its limitations, but if you are smart you can take the income you create and exponentially multiply its value in other ways, such as investing.

Each of us can tune into our natural strengths, look at how we can serve others and then become the best at what we do, which in turn makes us more valuable, which increases what we can charge or how many people we can impact. The better you are at something, the more people will be willing to invest in you. And when I say best, I don't mean best in comparison with others, it means you commit to being better than you were the day before. You are your only yardstick.

You are here for a reason and your expression of that ability makes you unique. Your whole life has been gearing you up, challenging you and helping you grow so that you can be the best version of you. Remember also, you are not confined to having just one purpose; you have multiple purposes, and your higher calling may not have anything linked to what makes you income. Your higher calling may be to stand up for animal rights or to spread the message of sustainability, build schools in Africa or fight against child trafficking. Your job may be the thing that provides you income so that you have energy and space to focus on the things that give your life meaning and purpose. Your life experiences have provided you with a wealth of knowledge, and that learning is valuable to others.

What have all your experiences over a lifetime prepared you for?

For me, suffering in my darkest times has armed me with a level of empathy for others that most do not have. I understand why people feel the way they do because I've been there. It's also made me more determined to support others and use my experiences of overcoming depression and anxiety to help others do the same.

I've had to deal with a lot in my life: finding out at nine years old that people close to me had been sexually abused, being bullied at school, suffering with depression and anxiety that I had no clue how to stop, experiencing not one but two divorces, watching my stepdad die from alcoholism, one brother survive cancer, one brother survive a brain aneurysm and stroke, not to mention seven heartbreaks and a shitload of hangovers. I am so sure there are millions of people on this planet who have been through way worse things, but it doesn't matter, because each of us go through our own journey and it will affect us in different ways.

These life experiences have shaped my personality and character in a profound way and have made me more resilient. I decided to take my pain and turn it into power. I know there are people in the world going through way worse things than me and, using my ability to pivot my perspective, I've decided to use it to help people in this world. Maybe that's something you feel called to do, or maybe not, but either way I want you to know that everything you have gone through has happened for a reason.

What pain have you been through that you can turn into power?

Maybe you can take your darkness and help bring light to others. I want to reiterate that we don't need to do something grand or extraordinary in our lives. But if we can help impact others, even in a small way, we are contributing to our own feeling of fulfilment. The most important thing is that you give your life some meaning as this has a correlation to your own happiness.

We all have a higher calling to make a difference in the world, to leave our footprint in the hearts of others. Whether that be in your family, where you work, your community, country or globally – there is someone waiting for *you to* help them.

I want you to take a moment now to really think about how you can make a difference in the world. One of my favourite tasks to give people to do is to get them to think about the world before money existed – a world where people could only exchange services for services. I want you to grab a piece of paper and write down as many things that you could do, however big or small, that could serve others. Take your time and really think about *everything* you could do for others, irrespective of what you would get paid for it.

37
Let There Be Light

I despise poorly lit rooms. They are literally one of the banes of my life. When someone tries to hand me an energy-saving lightbulb and expects me to live in darkness, I want to punch them. Light-bulbs are not created equal, they come in all shapes and sizes and what is quite fantastical about them is that you can screw a different bulb into the exact same electricity supply of one exact lampshade and the amount of light that comes out can be vastly different.

Stick a 10-watt bulb into the lampshade in my living room and I might as well not have it on. Buy a fancy schmancy LED bulb and – boom! – my house feels like it's been lit up like Blackpool pleasure beach. Same lamp, same electricity supply, different bulb.

Each of us has *the exact same supply* of incredible life-force energy coursing through us, but what determines how bright our life is, is the quality of our bulb, which symbolizes our thoughts. Humans that are operating from a lower level of thinking are stuck in a lower level of consciousness, only aware of what they see and what they experience with their five senses.

People with their LED bulbs have a higher level of conscious-ness, are in control of their thoughts and not only able to see more possibilities, but are able to shine. They can shed huge light on their life and see what is possible for them beyond what they can smell, hear, taste and touch. Those people also have the ability to shine light on others who are in darkness and offer a helping hand in seeing their own greatness. So how do we operate from the Soul each day? Well the first step is to stop operating in sur-vival mode.

Most of us go through life with a 10-watt bulb in and our mind cannot see the opportunities in front of us, because we are stuck trying to survive to meet our basic needs in life. Instead of seeing the million pounds of value we can offer, we buy into the story that we are not valuable to the world. When we operate from Soul, not Ego, we literally let the light flood in and start to see that life is for thriving not just surviving like a humanoid. Operating from the Soul means choosing not to live in fear, choosing to trust your intuition and choosing thoughts that are conducive to your brightest future. When we are tuned in, we can feel the stream of communication from the Universe guiding us to our *dharma*.

As a gift from me, I have created a special meditation that will help you connect with your spiritual self – that pure potential waiting to manifest into whatever the fuck you desire. Check it out on my website: <www.thisisyourdream.com/yolo>

When you give yourself the gift of shutting down the incessant chatter of the fear-based Ego in your mind, purpose starts to reunite with you like a long-lost friend. It never needed to be found, it was never lost. It's like when you shake a snow globe hard and you can't quite see the statue of Big Ben under the flurry of fake snow inside the plastic shell. As humans, we can end up spending our lives being shaken up like that snow globe. Your purpose however, is underneath the flurry of life, the constant stream of thinking and the perpetual 'doing'. We are human beings, not human doings, after all. You just gotta take a hot minute to let the snow settle, get present with this exact moment and you will see clearer than ever before what is underneath.

Why am I here and how can I make the most of this one life and make even a tiny footprint on this world?

Many people don't answer this question until later in life, but when they do, they realize that everything in life that was thrown at them – the good, the bad and the fucking ugly – was there to help them grow into the 2.0 version of themselves, so that they are ready to share their gifts. Your purpose may be small or it may be big – it doesn't matter – but whatever your Soul came here to do will unfold to you, once you put on a bigger bulb and let that snow settle.

38
Survival Mode

For years, every time I picked up the phone to my mum or stepdad and asked them how they were, the same word would come out. It wasn't 'Fine!' like most people's de facto cliché answer is. It was 'Surviving…'.

Well, we all have basic needs that we need to meet. We cannot be expected to create our best life if we are hungry or living on the streets. These survival needs are outlined in Abraham Maslow's Hierarchy of Needs, which is a widely regarded theory of motivation. In short, Maslow theorized that we won't fulfil our potential unless we meet these survival needs first. Then we are in the best position to self-actualize.

Self-actualization is a fancy word used in psychology that basically means the manifestation of one's potential, the fullest development of one's abilities and an utter appreciation for life. When an acorn self-actualizes, it has become a full-grown mighty oak. When we are stunted from self-actualization it causes an electric restlessness in our bodies resulting in feeling overwhelmed, frustrated and stuck. Self-actualization involves positive growth that gives life shape and meaning, including the development of spirituality and being able to tune into Universe FM on a daily basis.

Contrary to religion, which typically involves customs, beliefs, rituals and traditions, spirituality is highly personal and different for each of us.

Being spiritual to me refers to finding meaning and purpose in my life and connecting with the powerful non-physical part of me. It's a recognition that there's more to life than we can ever see and that there is a greater intelligence ever present, by my side, every goddamn step of the way.

Meeting our survival needs alone will never give us a long-lasting feeling of satisfaction in life, and in fact can induce anxiety if they aren't met. Think about how you feel when you get really hungry. My children get frustrated, on edge and angry. Sorry did I say children? I meant me! However, if I asked you a week later what you ate on Tuesday for lunch, you would probably struggle to recall. That's because who really cares what you ate last week – it does not create long-term satisfaction, it's just something you need to do in order to survive.

You can't become an oak tree without water, sun or good soil. We can't become the best version of ourselves without a roof over our heads and food in our bellies. We need to survive, and so operating at this level of life helps us navigate in the human, physical world. However, being fixated at this level of survival consciousness stops our Soul from growing, and keeps us feeling stuck and locked in fear.

Survival needs are at the bottom of Maslow's pyramid. At the top is the need to self-actualize, which involves growth and contribution to the world – these are needs of the spirit and what your Soul craves. When we meet those needs, they will give us long-lasting satisfaction and will keep us metaphorically filled up for life, unlike the Chinese all-you-can-eat buffet that you regret 20 minutes after. That electric restlessness that bubbles under your skin begins to dissipate, and peace will flood your body when you honour those spiritual needs.

When our life revolves around working to survive and everything we do is geared to meet our most basic needs for security, safety, love, belonging – and our need to feel good about ourselves rather than fulfilling our greatest potential and honouring our deepest desires – we have missed the point of life.

Your purpose is to do whatever it takes to fight past survival mode and to meet not just your Ego's needs, but your Soul's needs too. When people message me to thank me for helping them change their life, it's porn for my Soul. It fills me with joy and keeps me turned on and motivated to keep doing what I'm doing.

Unlike the Sunday roast I devoured last week, those messages will leave an imprint on my heart.

The way we move out of survival consciousness and into a higher level of awareness is to think about how we can meet our needs of growth and contribution. You need to want to identify your gifts and find your higher calling in life. This is also a guide toward figuring out the unlimited value you can offer the world. That is why I asked you earlier how you can be of service to others and how you can contribute to the world. We also need to make a commitment to keep growing as individuals emotionally, mentally and spiritually. When we stop growing, we get stuck. When we stop moving towards something bigger, we get that electric restlessness. That's because we are meant to keep growing.

Stop living just to survive.

Start living to thrive.

39
When You Know, *You Know*

'Do you really want your child to come into the world with all that noise?!'

Yes, that's what the midwife said to me during what were the most terrifying and painful moments of my life, as I gave birth to my second child and screamed in defiance at every moment.

I was prepared for this birth. I would get an epidural like my first child. I would abandon any need to be one of those mothers who remained calm and breathed like a goddess while her insides felt like they were being ripped out. I would happily numb myself waist down and Bob's your uncle!

There is one thing about labour and life – no amount of planning can prepare you for the shit hitting the fan, unforeseen obstacles and 40-minute labours. To say I was terrified was an understatement. From the minute I walked into that sterile hospital room at 10.40pm on the 26 February 2015 – which also happened to be my 29th birthday – I knew the baby was coming very soon.

However, the midwives told me that I was only 2cm dilated and I had a long way to go. Every minute became more and more unbearable, with each contraction engulfing my body like a tsunami of pain that I kept resisting. Every five minutes I begged them to check me again – 'I must be ready to push!'

'I cannot check you again as it can lead to infection. You still have a long way to go,' the midwife bluntly told me. I could tell from her energy she was tired and the whole time I was there I felt like I was somehow inconveniencing her by coming in to give birth that evening.

After another frantic guzzle of the gas and air, I threw up my birthday meal of spaghetti bolognaise. I wept in agony and begged for an epidural. The midwife checked me again at 11.45pm. 'You are 3cm dilated – you are officially in active labour.'

Active labour? What the fuck was the last hour of hell?

'There is only one anaesthetist on the ward,' she informed us. 'So I don't know if we can get you an epidural tonight, but we can try.'

I felt my insides curl up with every contraction and fear engulf every cell of being. I hadn't prepared for any other outcome. I cried and begged my mum to find me an anaesthetist as though she had some tiny black book of stand-by surgeons in case her daughter went into labour in a hospital where there was only one anaesthetist on the ward, who was otherwise engaged. *How dare he!*

Ten minutes later, what looked like a 12-year-old boy walked in and said he would give me an epidural. I was delirious and confused why they wouldn't give me a real doctor. But at this point I'd take a 12-year-old surgeon, just so I could get some respite (although I'm not sure he took it too well when I was asked why they let 12-year-old boys anaesthetize people!).

'This is a conspiracy,' I tried to whisper to my husband through my tears. 'They do not want to help me!' Rich held my hand and whispered in my ear. 'It's okay, they do want to help you – stop telling the doctor he's only 12 years old – he is a grown man, just a small grown man!'

I sat on the side of the bed and the doctor urged me to stay still. I flung my arms around my mother's neck as I had done as a child, hoping for solace, I felt intense pressure on my bowels and as if the evening couldn't get any worse, I genuinely believed I was about to shit myself.

'Mum, I really feel like I need to poo! Do not let Richard see!' My worst labour nightmare was about to unfold and I wanted to hold onto a morsel of dignity. I thought I had said it quietly, but the midwife overheard me and said she needed to check me before the doctor administered the epidural.

The problem with having an epidural the first time is that nobody tells you that feeling like you are about to shit yourself is the same feeling you get when the head is crowning and your body is ready to push the baby out.

Then it came – the words that no mother who is not prepared for a labour without pain relief wants to hear. 'The head is coming out.'

'No!! Give me that epidural. Pleeeeeasse!!'

I tried to close my legs in defiance. I screamed like a woman possessed. 'Give me the epidural, I cannot do this, I cannot do this.'

I feared for my life.

I feared for everything.

I wasn't prepared.

The pain felt like it would kill me and at one point I saw a bright white light – I genuinely believed in that moment, that I was dying.

This was what death was like.

'You can do this,' Richard said as he looked into my eyes and squeezed my hand in complete helplessness.

The good news is it only took two pushes and I did not shit myself. The bad news is that no one warned me that as the baby comes out, it feels like someone has stuck a hot poker right up your bits. That sting of fire as your baby enters the world.

40 minutes after the midwife told me I had only started labouring, my second beautiful daughter, Safia-Lily, was born into the world.

I cried and I swore the whole time, as my darling Safia made her way through the birth canal and out into the world and, while the midwife was more concerned about the noise I was making, she should have been worried about the noise the world was making. The noise that my darling child would end up being presented with every day of her life.

I held my new baby close to my chest, love filling up in me, erasing the pain, wiping away the horror of the last 40 minutes.

I was so terrified of labour that I had chosen not to prepare mentally. I chose to not even entertain the idea that I could give birth without pain relief.

I had decided I wouldn't have been strong enough, bold enough, brave enough to birth the child without numbing my body waist down.

I had been afraid of pain my whole life, afraid of heartbreak, afraid of parents not loving me, afraid that people at school didn't like me.

Scared that the boogeyman could jump out at any moment and rip my happiness away from me. That is the plague of anxiety.

I had tried to shield myself from so much pain my whole life, that when it came to one of the most incredible experiences of my life, instead of experiencing every moment despite the outcome, I broke down.

As humans we are taught to fear giving birth. I thought about why I was scared – it was because every single labour depicted on TV and films had taught me to be scared of it, instead of empowered by it. It truly is a miraculous thing that we women can grow and birth a brand new human into the world.

The next day in the shower, I wished I could do it again. I had done the thing that had scared me the most. Nothing else in the world had ever induced fear in me like labour and, against all my will, I was flung into facing my fears.

Face your fears, even if you do it kicking and screaming.

Face your fears even if there's ugly crying and snot.

Face your fears because everything you desire is on the other side of the fears.

Make a decision that you can do the crazy, the scary, the impossible.

There was no point in regrets, so with my third child, I made a completely different decision.

I set myself up for success and I gave birth to Amira-Jasmine at home with no pain relief. Yep, I chose that. And while I did at one point ask the midwife, who sat on the floor in my living room, if I could go into the kitchen to get a knife to end it – the whole experience was much calmer.

When I *knew* she was coming, I chose to not be afraid.

I chose to be present.

I chose to breathe.

I chose not to listen to the midwives who once again told me I was not far enough to push, and I got on all fours on my sofa, whipped off my bikini bottom and trusted my body.

This time the sting was a gentle reminder that it was almost over. And with one graceful push, I welcomed my third daughter into the world in complete silence. Yes, complete silence and peace.

I trusted the knowing in me.

I trusted my body.

I learned from experience instead of fearing it.

I embraced the unknown and the change in situation, which was there would be no baby born into the birthing pool we had spent hours filling up. No, she would start her reign on this planet from my sofa, and that was ok.

The unknown is scary, but the more we embrace it and build our resilience, the better we can stride through life. When we allow ourselves to experience every part of life, and lean into those experiences, we allow ourselves to fully live and learn.

Learning to trust your own intuition in a world where we are taught to rely on external information takes courage and practice because it involves fully taking on full responsibility for your thoughts, and your actions. Intuition is divine instruction, we just need to allow ourselves to be guided.

Just like I knew I was ready to push my baby, I *knew* I was going to be an author and get a book deal two years before it happened. It felt like electricity was circulating through my body when I heard Elizabeth Gilbert talk about getting a book deal in her book *Big Magic*. At that time I was driving and the sense of knowing penetrated every hair follicle on my body, causing each and every tiny hair to stand up. Sometimes the knowing is not such a visceral physical reaction, and can be a subtle nudge in your gut and a feeling of expansion within your body.

Part of uncovering your higher calling in this world is being able to listen and follow the nudges from your inner guidance system; to trust that divine instruction. It's funny that we believe that everything we need to know is outside us, when all the knowledge we have ever needed is right where you are. Beneath the chaos and noise of everyday life, deep beneath your skin and bones, is a place where your inner guidance system sits. The guide that gently nudges you into a space of knowing, a place where logic is not invited. Because sometimes knowing goes against every last bit of logic that our left brain tries to impose on us. This guidance is the life force and all its wisdom, and if you take time out of the chaos of life, you will feel it.

40

The Path Will Reveal Itself

It was while I was on maternity leave in 2013 with my first daughter, Layla-Rose, that I decided to revisit the whole manifestation thing. I purchased a brand-new A4 notepad, and proceeded to write on the first blank page: *I am so grateful for the £500 a month that I will earn that will help me stay home with my daughter*. At this point £500 a month would have been life-changing to us and would mean I wouldn't have to go back to a job I didn't like.

Within a few days I received an email titled *Want to make an extra £500 a month?* I was shocked and dubious. This was the first time I had ever seen something happen like this and wrote it off as a *coincidence*. However, something niggled in me (inner wisdom!), and I re-read the email and for a small cost you could invest in a course that taught you how to make money by claiming betting sites' bonuses.

It sounded too good to be true and also slightly ridiculous. I had never gambled in my life or signed up for a betting site, and just even mentioning this to Richard at the time came with palpable scepticism. I was disbelieving and yet curious, but my gut said do it. When a coincidence like this arises, don't ignore it. Ask yourself, 'What is the message here? What is the significance of this?' You don't need to go digging for the answers, trust that inner wisdom. Later that day I had made my first £20. If I did that every day, I'd make £500, which I went on to do.

When you have activated a visualization with emotion, and this is done unconsciously all the time, a yellow brick road to your very own Oz starts to lay itself. Neville Goddard coined the term the 'Bridge of Incidents' to describe the series of events that occur to bring about that which you desire. In short, once you have made up your mind about what you want, strategically orches-trated and perfectly aligned synchronicities will start to show up to help you get to your goal. Synchronicities are like on-purpose winks from the Universe and represent a collision of events where something other than the probability of chance is involved, and this confluence feels meaningful. It is an occurrence where needs are met, people are encountered, or things just come together perfectly just when we need them.

However, there is an important lesson here. The path will make itself clear to the next levels of the video game of life, but you need to take physical action. You need to meet the Universe half-way. This means following those signs and synchronicities, listen-ing to that internal wisdom and taking the inspired action that is required to make what you desire come to fruition in the physical world. Our lives are peppered with meaningful synchronicities that we can choose to embrace – the tricky part is simply learning how to spot them and interpret their messages.

That experience of following that email all the way through to making my first £500 was the start of an intimate and powerful journey of trusting that divine instruction, which to this day has been the best source of information to help me grow my business and my life.

However, there is a paradox to manifestation, and that is while we must take physical action in the physical world to bring to life our desires, we must equally surrender to the process. This is the difference between floating downstream in a beautiful river or swimming upstream against the tide. Surrender is allowing the unfoldment of your desires and trusting the process instead of pushing through. That's why taking the *right action* is crucial.

The right action feels good. The right action feels guided even when it doesn't feel logical. The right action does not drain you or cause resistance.

The right action isn't guided by fear. It also requires you to have unbounded faith that the outcome will manifest. If you spend each day questioning where your dreams are, you are doubting the

Universe and shifting your energy for peace and joy, to frustration and desperation. This throws you out of the vortex and onto the curb where you will be delaying the physical realization of what you want.

Faith is hard, because it requires us to trust in the unseen.

It forces us to relinquish the control that our Egos have been so accustomed to.

Catch how you speak about your desires, as your words are like a wand casting spells on your life. They are powerful at cementing the circuitry in your mind. Don't say 'I hope' or 'I wish' or 'I need'. Faith says 'I am' with confidence. When you can rise to a level of consciousness where you can say I AM, this is the place where miracles are made. When you decide to have a better future, the power of that decision will create quantum shifts in your reality and your energy will be in vibrational alignment; you become the magnet of your desire.

I am healthy.

I am wealthy.

I am in a loving relationship.

I am living *on purpose.*

'I am' shows faith and while it may be a physical lie in your 3D world right now, it is a spiritual truth. If you can see what you desire in your imagination, then you must know that your desire was put into *your* heart because it is meant for you. Your Soul knows what you are destined to do and that's why you can see it and feel it in your mind's eye.

Faith is necessary because it is the fuel that lights the fire and keeps the cog turning in the Universe. And there are moments where your faith is pushed to the very limit, like on 12 October 2019, where my whole world came crashing down in an instant.

41

Miracles

I wish I could erase the memory of Saturday 12 October 2019 from my memory. I walked in through the door after a hot yoga class and I noticed a missed call from my sister. I called her back.

'Leyth collapsed at the football match and he is now in brain surgery!'

She told me that my brother, who was in Budapest at the time helping at an EU conference on sustainability, had suddenly collapsed and was in brain surgery.

You know when someone gives you information that is so hard to process that you almost want to pass out because that would be easier – that honestly was how I felt. I had so many questions that I couldn't get answers to. *How and why did he go from collapsing at football to brain surgery?!*

I tried to breathe but just collapsed on my kitchen floor like a deflated balloon, as though the life from each of my limbs was sucked away. When I spoke to my mum, I knew it was serious.

I could barely make out what she was saying because she sounded like she was having a panic attack and hysterically crying all at the same time. My mother was a nurse and she had worked many years alongside brain surgeons and usually has a very matter of fact approach to any medical issues that arise. She is the mum who would send you to school no matter how unwell you felt because – unless your limb was hanging off – you were fine. This was scarily different. To hear her like this, barely being able to breathe through the tears, terror emanated through every cell in my body. *I'm going to lose my brother.*

I frantically booked flights for my mother and brother Henry to fly out on the next available flight. My mum almost couldn't

get on the flight. She was so hysterical at the airport that she threw
up at security and almost passed out and they said she wouldn't
be able to board unless she calmed down. Even writing this and
thinking of the pain she felt brings tears to my eyes. Any parent
knows that the prospect of losing a child is too unbearable to even
think about. As my mum and my other brother flew over there,
Leyth underwent a series of surgeries to save his life – at this point
the scariest part was that we still had no clue what was actually
wrong with him.

As the evening unfolded and my mother arrived at the hospital,
we were told that Leyth had a grade 4 aneurysm that had ruptured
– a medical rarity for someone of his age. This healthy 23-year-old
had a ticking time bomb in his head that none of us had known
about. It could have gone off at any time, anywhere, but it went
off in Budapest – which also happened to be the home and place
of one of the best aneurysm surgeons in the world.

I couldn't think.

I couldn't eat.

I was like a zombie staring into space, when I wasn't on phone
calls getting updates from my mother or updating my dad who
lived abroad now. I've never prayed so hard in my life. Every second I kept visualizing my brother laughing with me, seeing him
with my family at Christmas – *losing him was not even an option.*

When we heard that his second operation to stop the bleeding
had failed, I felt like someone had got a hammer and had thrown it
at me. *This wasn't meant to happen. This cannot happen.* Richard and I
collapsed on my living room floor, both holding each other crying
trying to process the information. But I couldn't process anything.
None of this made sense. If there was any time for this God my
mother and father believed in to pull his finger out – *this was it.*

They informed us that they couldn't operate again as it was too
risky, and that we had to pray that Leyth survived the night. None
of us slept as we all exchanged texts at every hour of the night.

The next day, the news got worse. The doctors told us that he
had suffered a stroke during the night and despite the dangers

they would need to immediately perform a third operation. My mother would have to sign a disclaimer because his rate of survival had dropped to just 30 per cent. My mum only had moments to make this life-changing decision – although there was no choice. She wept and sobbed on the phone making sure we were all okay with this decision. Of course we were. *It was this or lose him.*

We waited what seemed like a lifetime as the operation went through. 'They stopped the bleeding' Henry told me on the phone a few hours later. 'But his brain had bled so much that he has suffered great brain damage and he is paralysed down the whole of his right side.' We cried again. I called my dad and delivered the news through my tears. He was silent.

My brother, my best friend, the happiest, most loved person I knew, is now paralysed?! I cried at the thought that he wouldn't be able to dance, or run, or drive again, but if he was alive then we would make it work – *as long as he was alive.* He went through yet another surgery to put a stent in his ruptured aneurysm and the surgery was a bittersweet success. He was now in a coma and we waited anxiously for him to show us any sign that he was willing to be part of our world again. They told us it could be weeks for him to wake up. Weeks?! The wait was agonising.

Messages from across the world came for him – my brother was so popular and we had prayers coming in every minute from people across the globe. His best friends flew out to be with my mother and Henry as I also organized my flights out. I flew out to be with everyone the following day and seeing him lying there with tubes coming out of every part of his body was heartbreaking.

I held his hand, kissed his warm head and tried to hold back the tears. I asked him to listen to me as I read him a prayer. A miracle happened at that moment. He squeezed my hand and suddenly tears began trickling down his face. His eyes were closed but I knew he could hear me – *he couldn't possibly be brain dead?!* It was like he was trapped, wanting to communicate but couldn't quite figure out how. The hospital was very strict and only two hours a day were allocated to visitors and, since there were so many of us there, I decided to fly home to go get my family and we would come back out in two days.

When I arrived back with my whole family, my dad also flew in and more of Leyth's friends – in fact there were 22 of us out there at one point all praying hard for our boy to wake up. As I was packing my bags to fly out, I received a call from my mother. 'He's opened his eyes Noor! He's awake!' He had opened his eyes and his first words to my mum and brother were 'Fuck the system, get me out of here.'

It felt like he had won an Olympic medal ten times over and we were all there to celebrate on the front row. I had not felt happiness like it in all of my life – he wasn't brain dead. It was a high that I'd never felt before – a celebration of all celebrations. I couldn't wait to board the plane and hold him in my arms.

I will never forget standing at his bedside, with my mum and my dad, all of us there looking over at him. He asked me 'Am I dying?' because this was the first time all five of us had been in the same room in 20 years.

'No baby,' my mum said, 'You are definitely not!'.

He couldn't move much of his body, and when he came down off the four-day morphine high (which honestly had kept us entertained because of the amount of shit he was talking), the doctors told him he wouldn't be able to walk.

If there's something that we have become really good at in my family, it's NOT believing in the man in the white coat, because – with all the best intentions – doctors only tap into the physical world and my brother is an ancient Soul. He was teaching me about the world being energy at 16 years old and I remember thinking 'Who is this weirdo?'. The fact that his first words as he woke up from a seven-day coma were 'Fuck the system' was like the message I had needed to hear my whole life.

My dad told him to imagine what he would do when he got out of there. Leyth closed his eyes and said 'I'm surfing in Bali'. My dad told him to imagine that every day and, over the 22 hours that my brother was alone and stuck in that hospital bed, he would surf, he would run, he would do all he wanted in his imagination. Not being able to walk was not an option.

Four weeks later, against any medical logic, he was walking. One year later he had trained for an ironman and was in the best shape of his life. He had beaten all the odds, using the power of his thought. The doctors said they have never seen anything like it and he will forever be the example of how thought can change your life.

My mum and dad will tell you that God saved my brother. I will tell you that the Universe supported his healing through the collective thoughts, prayers and energy we put out there. I really don't care what you think, but by simply having the belief it's possible, miracles can happen.

What my brother did was a miracle to many. He achieved the impossible, but this is what the likes of Dr Bruce Lipton and Dr Joe Dispenza have been sharing for decades. What we need to understand is that the non-physical part of us has the ability to heal the physical part of us, and by using our imagination we can literally change the gene expression in our physical bodies.

If I build an image of me as a happy, relaxed person, I can live like that. If I build an image of being wealthy, I can live like that. If I build an image of me surfing when I've been told I am paralysed, there's a really huge chance that one day I will be able to do just that. Miracles like this have been documented time and time and time again. We just need to believe in the magic like we did as children.

42

Not-So-Comfort Zones

I had my head buried far into the scratchy hostel bed pillow, hoping that none of the 20 random people in the dorm could hear me sobbing. *What the fuck was I doing?*

It was scary enough that I'd decided to pack my life into a big pink suitcase and take a one-way ticket to Australia alone, but how the hell did I get roped into camping on an island where training on how to save yourself from being mauled by dingoes was a thing?!

I'd never gone camping before and the first time would be with a group of strangers on a random island for three nights in Australia – and I might possibly not make it out with all my limbs. This was the epitome of pushing myself out of my comfort zone.

It's actually quite a funny story of *how* I ended up at that sad moment, crying into a scratchy hostel pillow in a dorm full of backpackers who were happy to dice with death on Fraser Island. Well, what do you do in life if you don't know what to do with your life? Travel! I made the bold decision after G and I broke up that after my season in Greece, I would escape 'real life' for as long as possible and see the world.

I got on a plane on 27 December 2008, by myself, and ended up sitting with a lovely chap who enjoyed drinking Bloody Marys just as much as I did. With hindsight, I feel awfully sorry for anyone that was in our cabin, because for almost 19 hours we talked and drank and talked louder and drank more. We giggled when we got reprimanded and the steward kept sneaking us more mini bottles. We were two strangers, catching up on decades of life, at 40,000 feet in the sky.

The funniest part was, he had sat in the wrong seat, so this story could have been very different. I arrived in Australia drunk and was met by a guy I'd had a bit of a holiday romance with, a few months earlier in Thailand. And of course, I'd already mentally planned out our future and our Aussie children – I already mentally explained to my mum that I'd been leaving the UK for good, because I'd finally found 'the one'. I had of course, inevitably, started to fall for him even though I'd known him for like five minutes, but since you now know me a little better, you will have come to see that I'd have fallen in love with a giraffe if it gave me five minutes of attention. To be fair, I wish I had fallen for a giraffe, because the Aussie boy turned out to be an utter prick.

Just ten days later, I was crying down the phone to my mum feeling exceptionally sorry for myself and insisting that I should just get on a plane home. My mum quite rightly reminded me that I'd gone there for me and to enjoy myself and to stop letting 'silly boys' affect me like this. *He wasn't silly mother, he was my future husband who had now abandoned me to fend for myself in Australia.*

At that point, plane-guy messaged me and as I explained how heartbroken I was again, he told me to fly to meet him and his mate in Queensland. So I fled Melbourne and went. Plane-guy booked us three nights camping on Fraser Island with dingoes and demonic flies that buzz so loud it gave you chills and were known for biting chunks out of your arms.

'It'll be fun and character building,' he said. You know what? It was. It was strange spending three nights sleeping in a tent close up to a guy I met on a plane just 14 days earlier. It was super strange to have to cook and eat with complete strangers, and it was horrifying going to sleep thinking that any moment a dingo would walk straight into the tent and make hors d'oeuvres out of your toes. But it was character building and, while it took me everything not to fall for plane-guy too, I made it out alive, with both legs and a slightly more mended heart.

You see, in life we've got to do the scary shit. We need to embrace the unknown with enthusiasm and trust that all will work out just fine.

When we do something so freaking out of our comfort zone, we get those butterflies in our stomach and that fear trying to stop us moving forward, like a bouncer at the front of the queue of the club you so desperately want to get into because it's bloody freezing outside and you are completely inappropriately dressed for January.

Fear is wonderful – it helps us to swim as fast as we can when we see a fin slowly moving towards us in the sea, and it helps us run as quick as we can if a bear walks into our hotel (this literally happened in the hotel next to us in Vermont!) and it stops you from doing stupid stuff like jumping off a 100 foot cliff.

However, fear can and will show up uninvited in the dreams we have of our future, demanding that it takes the front seat. The nature of life is that it's uncertain and, therefore, fear is a natural part of navigating that unknown. None of us can know what will happen next and spending our life trying to figure out those outcomes is what causes us more resistance and more fear.

Our bodies are designed to react to fear as we confront the unknown. That's because when we rip off the Mulberry handbag, the Rolex watch, the Nike trainers and Ann Summers underwear, underneath we are just animals. The reason we feel fear is because when we embark on something new, our brain is diligently pulling up a list of all the risks and, since it's the chief security officer in charge of keeping you safe in life, it will overreact to the unknown, because it cannot accurately predict what is coming.

The thoughts of what will go wrong will start to creep in as a result of past experiences where you embarked on something new and it didn't work, and that creates the same uneasy feeling in your body. The feeling is a result of your adrenals doing their work and pumping the stress hormone cortisol around the body.

As I shared earlier, watching television can have a profound effect on stress levels in our bodies, even when we logically know that what is happening on the screen is not actually happening to us. The same happens when we worry about the future – our brain doesn't know if it's real or imagined and our body reacts accordingly. Let that land. We can feel a false sense of stress that can activate false thoughts. Worrying about an event that 'may' happen is not the same as thinking about something that has happened. It's thinking about something that *could* happen, and the reason we feel anxiety is because the focus is on what will go wrong.

Let me prove this to you right now. I want you to close your eyes and imagine that you are going downstairs to your kitchen, grabbing a lemon, cutting the lemon and then sucking on the lemon in your mind's eye. Do that now. What happens? I bet you my bottom dollar that you started to have a physical reaction to what you imagined. This is proof that, if you allow yourself to believe the thoughts of all the risks in the future, your body will react accordingly, and you start the negative feedback loop that keeps you in that stressful state of being.

I'll never forget when I got onto stage for my TEDx Talk. I was terrified that people would notice that my legs were shaking so violently. I don't usually get such bad nerves when I speak on stage, but this was different. I had only found out 48 hours before that I was going to be delivering a talk and this is something that I'd written down as a goal just 14 days earlier. In the space of 14 days, my desire had come to fruition and I had to write, rehearse and deliver this talk that would be filmed and put onto the wild, wild web forever, in less than two days. This is the power of writing your goals down. Don't ever leave goals whirling around in your head – write this stuff down! Every time I felt sick and scared, I reminded myself *why* I was doing the talk. I was doing it to inspire people and to make an impact. It wasn't just about me, but the students I would speak in front of.

That's why we must focus our attention on rewards. Where your attention goes, energy flows. What you focus on grows and shows up more in your life. Once you are clear on that vision for your future, your dreams and your goals, learn to lose yourself in those desires; feel yourself there as vividly as possible. Think about all the rewards and allow those thoughts and feelings to start creating a different state of being, one not of fear. Everything you desire is on that other side of your comfort zone, you need to be brave enough to take that step out with unadulterated faith.

Faith is the antidote to fear but, annoyingly, you can't pick up a bottle at the pharmacy so you can start popping them faith pills and overcome fear. Faith is a muscle and it needs to be strengthened. Once you have planted the seed of your desire into that quantum field, you can practise having faith and confidence that it will appear – then you have done your part. Don't shit in your vortex by worrying whether they will come to fruition – that simply is not your business and will stop the seed from blooming. Your purpose demands faith from you, to step into your higher calling and to do your something big.

You need to remember that and how powerful you are so that you can take that vision and manifest it in reality. There will be fuck-ups on the way to transforming your life and moments where you fall over and wish the world would suck you up. But stop living in fear of what others will say – they simply do not matter.

Be excited about stepping out of your comfort zone for the growth it will bring you. Everything you desire is on the other side of your comfort zone! Embrace the uncomfortable moments like you would someone you love. Those moments are your greatest teacher. You do *not* need to get it right or perfect. In fact, make it messy and realize that you can pick up those pieces after. Making mistakes gives you opportunities to grow, opportunities to get comfortable with being uncomfortable. This is the greatest and most liberating gift we can give ourselves. When you go for your dreams, step into your purpose and take ownership of your life, you will give others permission to do the same. And together we can start helping humanoids become human again.

I spent my teens and twenties caged into a life that made me abandon who I truly was at my core. I was suffocated by all the 'shoulds' and knew I was meant for more. My thirties taught me how to make life count. It taught me to honour each day because we only have one chance.

So what makes people truly fulfilled? Is it love, family, success? Or is it finding out who you *really are*? Finding out what you are truly made of, so you know your purpose here on earth and your connection to the Universe. I believe that life is a game and it has its rules and its aims. The rules can't be changed nor can they be broken. The whole purpose is to learn the rules and enter the playing field of your mind to create a life of your own design. The rules are simple but it takes us a lifetime to truly be able to apply them and master our thoughts – this I believe is our greatest purpose and the key to true fulfilment. Becoming aware of our daily mental activity and choosing to take control is our purpose.

I want my children to live in a world where they believe they have the choice to live their own lives on their own terms, not to be dictated by an invisible system that keeps them trapped in a limited life.

I want that for you too and I hope the pages in this book have helped you to wake up and see that life is for the taking, when you decide to take it.

Together we can start to wake up the world; together we can make a difference to how people feel and raise the collective vibration of the world. We have a responsibility to our Souls to evolve. I think we all need more joy and freedom, don't you?

Oh and don't forget to shake that miraculous booty of yours. You are a miracle – so go do some miraculous things. You only have one life after all and it's time to make it fucking count.

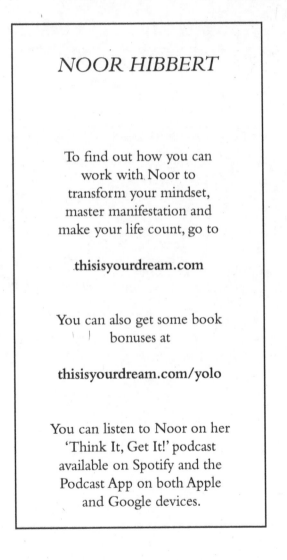

NOOR HIBBERT

To find out how you can
work with Noor to
transform your mindset,
master manifestation and
make your life count, go to

thisisyourdream.com

You can also get some book
bonuses at

thisisyourdream.com/yolo

You can listen to Noor on her
'Think It, Get It!' podcast
available on Spotify and the
Podcast App on both Apple
and Google devices.